Stan & Jan Berenstain

# DOWN A SUNNY DIRT ROAD

## AN AUTOBIOGRAPHY

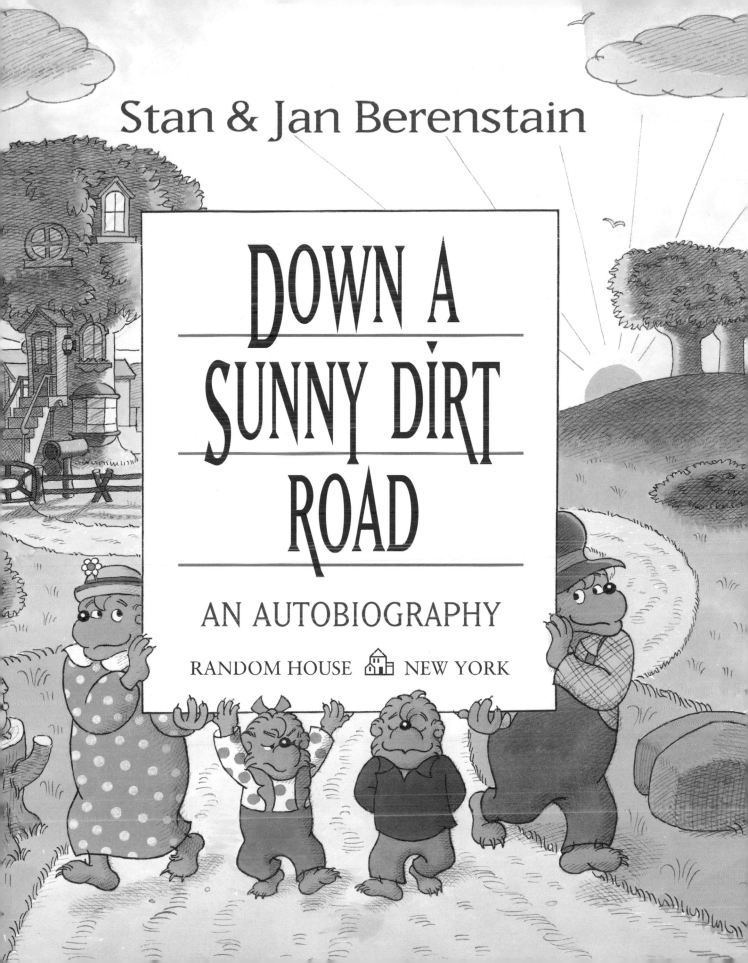

Stan & Jan Berenstain

# DOWN A SUNNY DIRT ROAD

## AN AUTOBIOGRAPHY

RANDOM HOUSE 🏠 NEW YORK

*For our progeny,*
*heretofore and hereafter.*

Copyright © 2002 by Berenstain Enterprises, Inc.
All rights reserved under International and Pan-American Copyright Conventions.
Published in the United States by Random House Children's Books,
a division of Random House, Inc., New York, and simultaneously in Canada
by Random House of Canada Limited, Toronto.

www.randomhouse.com/kids
www.berenstainbears.com

*Library of Congress Cataloging-in-Publication Data*
Berenstain, Stan, 1923–
Down a sunny dirt road / by Stan & Jan Berenstain.
   p.   cm.
SUMMARY: In alternating chapters Stan and Jan Berenstain, creators of the Berenstain Bears,
tell their own stories from early childhood until their marriage, then continue the tale together
to the present day.
ISBN 0-375-81403-5 (trade) — ISBN 0-375-91403-X (lib. bdg.)
1. Berenstain, Stan, 1923– Juvenile literature.   2. Berenstain, Jan, 1923– Juvenile literature.
3. Authors, American—20th century—Biography—Juvenile literature.
4. Berenstain Bears (Fictitious characters)—Juvenile literature.
5. Children's stories—Authorship—Juvenile literature.
[1. Berenstain, Stan, 1923–  2. Berenstain, Jan, 1923–  3. Authors, American.]
I. Berenstain, Jan, 1923–  II. Title.
PS3552.E6997 Z46   2002   813'.54—dc21   [B]   2001048317

Printed in the United States of America   First Edition   10 9 8 7 6 5 4 3 2 1

RANDOM HOUSE and colophon are registered trademarks of Random House, Inc.

# Stan & Jan Berenstain

# DOWN A SUNNY DIRT ROAD

## AN AUTOBIOGRAPHY

# EARLY STAN

JAN AND I WERE HEADED DOWNTOWN to my parents' fiftieth-anniversary party at the Barclay Hotel in Center City, Philadelphia. Jan's parents had been married for more than fifty years. Jan and I would go on to achieve a fifty-year marriage as well.

Perhaps researchers will identify a long-marriage gene someday. It will probably be located a couple of notches up the double helix from the early-memory gene.

I had been told I would be expected to "say a few words" at the celebration. There's nothing like a trip to your parents' fiftieth and the pressure of having to "say a few words" to trigger memory. But what to say? I'd have to be very careful. It would be an emotional affair, and I hate to see a grown man cry—especially if it's me.

A scheme came to me—one I thought I could handle. It came to me as a vista of addresses: 5656 Pentridge, 5514 Ridgewood, 5410 Chestnut, 7163 Marsden, 4239 Frankford—all the places I'd lived in Philadelphia back to when I was a fat-kneed little kid riding a tricycle out in front of my grandmother Nelly's Army and Navy Store on Frankford Avenue. . . .

It was 1927 and I was four years old. Nelly's Army and Navy Store stood under the "el," the elevated train structure that dominated Frankford Avenue. The Willys Knight Agency was on one side. (The Willys Knight was the snub-nosed little car that they gave away at the movies like dishes, which were the usual movie giveaway.) Vitacollona's Shoe Repair Shop was on the other side, and up the street were Torpy's (the florist), Bockman's Oyster House, and the corner firehouse, where I frequently made a pest of myself and where I was allowed to pet the cat.

Stan riding his tricycle in the small square across from his grandmother's Army and Navy Store. The "el," the Willys Knight Agency, and unemployed people on park benches in background.

Nelly, my widowed paternal grandmother, lived behind the store.

My mother, Rose, my father, Harry, and I lived over the store. My father, who was seldom home, traveled as a member of a store-opening crew for Sears, Roebuck.

Up on the third floor was a sickroom where a wraithlike woman lay abed. She was my maternal grandmother.

Though I was only four, I had the run of the store, which my mother managed, and the block from the Willys Knight Agency up to the firehouse. Behind the store was a yard where my mother hung clothes out to dry on a long clothesline supported by notched poles called clothes props. They were very long, and it seemed to me that if you could lash eight or ten of them together, you could knock up against the sky.

But even the most logical and well-thought-out theories must be put aside when serious doubt is eventually cast upon them.

At five, I was in the store drawing a cat—I was in my cat period at the time—when I heard a hue and cry. I ran outside. People were pointing up at the sky. I looked up. Crossing what was visible of the sky through the elevated train structure was a long, slim, silver cigar. "It's a zeppelin," explained the mechanic from the Willys Knight Agency. "It's the *Graf Zeppelin*."

It was clearly much higher than any number of clothes props could ever have reached. Reluctantly, I crossed the idea of lashing clothes props together off my list of things to do.

I was inspired by the great silver cigar. I put aside cats and entered into my zeppelin period. I drew zeppelins on every sur-

Stan's parents, Rose and Harry Berenstain.

DOWN A SUNNY DIRT ROAD

face I could find: brown paper bags, shirt cardboards, scraps of paper.

But just as Picasso exhausted his blue period and moved on to his rose period, I came to the end of my zeppelin period. I was about to enter a new period.

One day the mood at 4239 Frankford Avenue abruptly turned dark and dour. Uncles and aunts gathered. Everybody was speaking in hushed tones. My maternal grandmother had, after a long illness, died in the third-floor room. I was underfoot. Pop, my maternal grandfather, volunteered to take me for a walk.

We'd hardly started when something in the window of Vitacollona's Shoe Repair Shop caught Pop's eye. It was a display. It consisted of two shoes: one big enough for a giant and one small enough to fit my foot. Behind the shoes was a display of photographs. Pop explained that Mr. Vitacollona had made the shoes—

the big one in honor of Primo Carnera, an enormous Italian prize-fighter famous for his size 24 shoe, the small one for purposes of dramatic comparison. I didn't fully understand Pop's explanation, but I got the general idea. I certainly understood the photographs. They showed Mr. Carnera in a variety of poses, all having to do with prizefighting: smiting opponents with great gloved fists, having his hand held up by a referee, and just glowering. I had found my next subject. It was Primo Carnera.

When we returned from our walk, I began drawing Mr. Carnera with my usual medium, big red marking crayon, on my usual surfaces—brown paper bags, shirt cardboards, and scraps of paper.

I didn't know it at the time, but they were preliminary drawings for a larger work.

The aunts and uncles departed.

The pall lifted.

Things got back to normal—except for the arrival of men in white overalls, carrying ladders, buckets, long-handled brushes, and rolls of paper.

They went up the stairs to the third-floor room.

After a few days the men in white overalls left.

One day, shortly after their departure, my mother was in the store waiting on a flurry of customers, Grandmother Nelly was in the recesses of her living quarters, and I, big red marking crayon in hand, was climbing the stairs to the third-floor room.

What I found was a large, empty room with four walls newly papered with pale pink figureless wallpaper.

No Sistine Chapel, no post office, no Altamira Cave ever cried out more loudly for decoration.

Limited only by my limited stature, I proceeded to decorate those walls with a never-ending frieze of Primo Carnera in action.

In those days spanking wasn't frowned upon nearly as much as was scribbling on newly papered walls.

Without going into details, I will say only that I suffered for my art.

EARLY STAN

# EARLY JAN

I AM REMINDED BY CHECKING MY BIRTH CERTIFICATE that I was born at Woman's Hospital in West Philadelphia to my then twenty-eight-year-old mother, whose husband was thirty-three and whose doctor was a woman.

I don't have to be reminded that the year was 1923 or that I was named Janice Marian Grant after the title of a book by Paul Leicester Ford, *Janice Meredith,* and after my mother, Marian.

The book was given to my father, Alfred James Grant, by the Red Cross as he embarked on his one and only tour of duty as a radio operator on the battleship USS *Delaware* at the end of World War I in 1918. He gave the book to my mother on his return along with an engagement ring. She wore the ring secreted in her bosom on a long chain so she wouldn't lose her job as a stenographer for an importing firm.

Her educational background included high school and a year or so in stenographer school, which meant she could take short-hand, type, and operate a punch card machine. The punch card machine was used to punch holes in specific positions on cards to represent data, which would be fed into a mechanical computer. This was how her office translated and recorded bills of lading that came with foreign shipments.

My father's educational background was spotty, but formidable in the areas of his special interests. He learned carpentry from his father, who, sadly, became an alcoholic after Dad's mother died when he was twelve or so. His two older sisters went to live with an aunt, and he was put in an orphanage. He ran away and went back

A professional photograph of Jan at one.

to live and work with his father, whose health was deteriorating. He got books and lessons from the International Correspondence School and did very well in math, engineering, and draftsmanship. When his father died, he continued working but also went to night school at Drexel University for an architecture and engineering course and at the Philadelphia Museum School of Industrial Art for drawing and painting.

When Mom and Dad married, he teamed up with her father, Ambrose Beck, who was also a carpenter. They shared his handsome three-story row house on Forty-eighth Street near Market and made him a grandfather with the birth of my older brother, Al Jr. I came along two years later but remember very little about the four years of my life I lived there. I remember a front-door vestibule with a frosted glass inner door and half-walls of brown enameled panels pressed all over with bumpy curlicues. Al and I would shut ourselves in there pretending it was a playhouse. He marched the clay animals he made in kindergarten around the braided mat on the floor, and I traced the curlicues on scraps of vellum retrieved from the wastebasket by Dad's drafting table. I must have been fascinated with curlicues, because I also remember trying to trace the design cut into the mohair pile on our sofa. It didn't work. So I modified my approach by reproducing the sofa curlicues via a series of pencil point holes in the vellum. The popping noises this technique produced were quite satisfying to a four-year-old.

When Dad designed and built a house in the suburbs for the president of Garrett-Buchanan, a big Philadelphia paper company, Granddad

Jan's parents, Marian and Alfred Grant. Al was a Radioman First Class on the battleship USS *Delaware* during World War I.

retired and used his skills in the less demanding work of maintaining his properties. Besides owning the Forty-eighth Street house, he owned a property nearby on Market Street. It consisted of a mechanic's garage and storefront with living quarters behind and above. Mom used her skills in office work for him and Dad.

Soon we all moved out to the suburbs into a new semi-detached house, which meant we had windows all along one side as well as in front and back. This house was about the same size as the old house, but it had an attic instead of a third floor, grassy front and back yards, and a driveway up the side leading to a semi-detached garage. The garage became Dad's workshop, and we became the first kids on Stanley Avenue—maybe in all of Manoa—to have a custom-made swing in the backyard. There were all of five other kids on Stanley Avenue, and they were all boys. They lined up with us beside the tall swing structure to take turns. Al and

I learned a dangerous new sport from them. We pumped up the swing as high as we could, adjusted our grip so that our elbows were inside the ropes, pointing forward—and jumped off. Then we checked our footprints in the dirt where we landed and tried again and again to outleap each other. We ended up with stinging feet, shaky knees, and grubby hands, but I felt great—I was one of the boys.

My only girl company at that time was my two dolls. I spent a lot of time with them when I was indoors. One was a Mama doll with wavy brown hair like my mom's, so even though she cried, "Ma-ma! Ma-ma!" like an upset little kid, to me she was my other doll's mother. My other doll was an infant with a china head. She was an adorable bald little thing dressed in several long petticoats and a christening gown. Once or twice I christened her too hard and had to wait until Christmas for a new head.

Since there was no kindergarten at Manoa Elementary School, my preschool year was different from Al's. While he was in second grade, I was home learning all sorts of useful and artistic things.

Generally, children that young have such good eyesight that they often focus on fascinating items of small scale around the house and on their even smaller-scale details. Granddad had a couple dozen teaspoons from the Sesquicentennial Exhibition that had the names of different states and their elegantly designed seals embossed on the handles. He was happy to identify

Jan with her older brother, Alfred Jr., and her younger brother, Charley.

**EARLY JAN**

each one by name over and over again as I studied the images of each miniature picture. The pictures became the names of the states to me, and I could soon recite them all for my mother as if I were reading. Something related to the process of learning to read must have been going on—after all, the first alphabet was pictures.

Dad had a locked bookcase with glass doors that contained his ICS books, a set of illustrated Ridpath's *History of the World*, a *Cyclopedia* set, and lots of illustrated novels, including his prized edition of *Alice's Adventures in Wonderland* and *Through the Looking-Glass*. One of his favorite artists was John Tenniel, and because he let me draw at his drafting table that year like a fellow artist instead of on the floor like a little kid, he decided to unlock the bookcase and let me look at all the wonderful pictures. He took *Alice* out first.

In addition to the many Tenniel black-and-white illustrations, there were four color plates protected by tissue. I admired them immensely, and he left the book out for me to look at and for daily

readings. Somewhere between Alice's playing croquet with the Queen of Hearts and her talking to the live flowers, this "fellow artist" could resist the tempting tissues no longer and traced the White Knight onto one of them with a 2B drawing pencil (very black). I didn't get spanked—Dad must have understood the urge—but I knew he didn't appreciate the desecration of a favorite book, because he sat me on a high stool by his drafting table while he removed the tissue with his straight razor and painstakingly replaced it before reading on.

On my sixth birthday in the summer of that year, Aunt Bernadine, one of Mom's older sisters, gave me *A Child's Garden of Verses,* by Robert Louis Stevenson, with illustrations by Jessie Willcox Smith. I had a copybook with plain pages to draw in by then and was inspired by Jessie to intersperse my larger works with spot drawings—specifically, long-stemmed flowers with faces in them.

Aunt Bernie also brought along my older cousin Anne's first book of piano lessons, which she had completed. We unlocked Granddad's old upright and wound up the stool, and I started in on finger exercises. I remember thinking that learning to play the piano would make me ambidextrous like Anne, but my right hand was the star and my left hand never caught up.

Later that summer I was invited to sleep over at Anne's house in Upper Darby for a week while Al went off to visit our boy cousins in New Jersey. It was the first time either of us had the

experience of being away from home, and we both welcomed it. He reported having quite an adventure—being taken to the Lakehurst Naval Air Station, where he saw the *Graf Zeppelin*. It was so big that its mammoth nose and mooring mast stuck out of one end of the dirigible hangar, which was considerably mammoth itself.

I had an adventure, too. Anne, being three years my senior, enjoyed having a "little sister" to play with and take places. When Saturday came, she begged her mother to let her take me to the movies with her friends. *Daddy Long Legs* was playing at the Rivoli, one of three theaters we could walk to. At six years old, I saw my first scary movie.

The scary part was a dark opening scene that showed the three-quarter back view of a huge wing chair with long black-trousered legs sticking out in front. Shadows cast by the light of a fire in the fireplace were even longer and blacker. Anne was surprised when I started to scream and put her hat over my eyes. I peeked out from time to time with little comprehension of what

was going on, but the scary scene stayed with me. I had nightmares afterward as well as an aversion to movies—any movies—for a long time.

(A few years later on a subsequent visit, Anne and her friends wanted to see the new mystery at the Tower. That's when I saw my second scary movie, *Mystery of the Wax Museum*. There was a lot of screaming at that movie, and it wasn't just me.)

There was an air of excitement when Al and I returned to Manoa with our Jersey and Upper Darby relatives. Waiting were Mom, Dad, and Granddad . . . *and* a new baby brother! It was a complete surprise. I don't know about Al, but I had no idea where babies came from—and they never told me. Because dear Charley was in a basket, I assumed he had appeared by magic like baby bunnies at Easter. Besides, there was a baby in a basket in *Alice,* which was documented in an unforgettable Tenniel pen-and-ink drawing. What else did I need to know? Wherever they came from, they came in baskets—just like ours did.

EARLY JAN

# SCHOOL DAYS: STAN

I STARTED KINDERGARTEN at Alexander Hamilton Elementary School, which was six blocks from 4239 Frankford Avenue. My mother hired fourth grader Tony Vitacollona to take me to school. The fee was ten cents a day. But he insisted that he be paid each morning in pennies. Tony needed pennies to feed his gambling habit; he was addicted to pitching pennies. Penny pitching was a popular form of juvenile gambling, which involved standing behind a line near a wall and tossing pennies to see whose could come closest to the wall. The pitcher of the coin that came closest took all the pennies. There was always a game in progress on the way to school, and Tony always participated—sometimes at such length that we were late for school.

Lateness at Alexander Hamilton Elementary School was a crime punishable by having to sit on the late bench and get bawled out by Mr. Brody, the principal. Mr. Brody got very worked up over lateness.

To this day, I have such an aversion to being late that I make the early bird look like the ten o'clock scholar.

One day my father surprised my mother by showing up at the store at midday. He sat her down and told her he'd been laid off. Sears was cutting back. It was the Depression. They weren't opening any more stores. They kept only a couple men on. Why had they let him go? "I guess it's because I don't wear a homburg like Hoover."

I had a general idea what "laid off" meant; I had no idea what a "homburg" or a "Hoover" was. But I knew that something momentous had happened.

Things continued to happen. Events piled on events. Though my father now slept and had supper at home, he walked to the corner every morning and took the el downtown. "He's looking for a job," explained my mother. Why doesn't he just stay here and work in the store? I wanted to know. My mother smiled, drew me close, and said, "This place wouldn't keep a pussycat alive." Then there was Pop. He had lost his little Columbia Avenue haberdashery. *How do you lose a store?* I wondered.

While the world was closing in on my parents, it was opening up for me.

I had learned to read. I no longer needed to have the comics read to me. I could read them myself.

Comics were the popular entertainment of the day—for me, the entirety of popular entertainment. I'd only been to one movie. It was about "The War." It made a big impression on me, principally because the kindly disabled German general for whom prisoner of war Gary Cooper was a manservant had a collection of military dioramas peopled with toy soldiers. They were the most beautiful and desirable objects I'd ever seen. I wanted them. I needed them. My little soul cried out for them.

**SCHOOL DAYS: STAN**

Later, when things looked up, I got some toy soldiers. I got them for Christmas. Yes, Christmas. Not that we weren't Jewish. My grandparents—the lot of them—were Jewish enough to be pogrommed out of the Ukraine. But my playmates Albert and Marie Vitacollona got presents for Christmas. Why couldn't I? It seemed a reasonable request to my mother. Not only were Christmas presents forthcoming, but stockings were hung by the chimney with care on Christmas Eve.

But my mother drew the line at having a tree. The Vitacollonas had a beautiful tree.

"Mommy," I said, "you oughta see Vitacollonas' Christmas tree! It's really pretty."

"I'm sure it is."

"Can we have one, Mommy?"

"No."

"Why not?"

"We just can't."

"*Why* can't we have a Christmas tree, Mommy?"

"Because we're Jewish! That's why!"

And, of course, we were. Our family had been as Jewish as we could be for as far back as anybody could remember, notwithstanding that neither of my parents nor any of their siblings ever had any religious training—except for Eddy, my father's youngest brother. In a concession to propriety, he was sent to cheder. But the experiment was short-lived. When the rabbi saw fit to take a stick to him, Eddy floored him with a punch to the jaw.

Gary Cooper wasn't interested in the toy soldiers. He preferred to toy with the old general's young wife, Helen Twelvetrees.

"What are they doing, Mommy?"

"They're kissing. Shh!"

"Why are they kissing, Mommy?"

"*Shhh!*"

But I wasn't quite as dumb as I was making out.

I knew a little bit about the boy-girl thing. I'd learned it from the funny papers. Buck Rogers, my favorite comic hero, had a girlfriend, Wilma Deering. Harold Teen had Lillums. Dick Tracy had Tess Trueheart. Joe Palooka had Anne Howe. (Get it? I didn't, until I was eleven.) Tillie the Toiler had Mac (who was half her size). Olive Oyl's significant other, Popeye, offered wisdom as well as romance and fisticuffs. His oft-repeated credo—"I yam what I yam and that's all what I yam!"—still resonates down the decades.

One day I came home from school to find that Nelly's Army and Navy Store was "Closed Until Further Notice." I banged on the locked door. My mother let me in. As we walked through the darkened store, she explained that something wonderful had happened. My father had gotten a job. He was going to work at Polikoff's Army and Navy Store in downtown Philadelphia. "Now we don't have to keep this damn store open. And best of all, Nelly's gone to live with Aunt Bessy for a while."

That wasn't all. My parents, aunts, and uncles had chipped in and bought Pop a new business. It was the newsstand concession in the lobby of the Windsor Hotel, between Tenth and Eleventh on Filbert. And further, we would be going downtown to help Pop out on Saturdays.

Stan's maternal grandfather, Charles "Pop" Brander, behind the counter of his newsstand in the lobby of the Windsor, a theatrical hotel in Philadelphia.

Before going to the hotel, we used to stop off at Leary's Used Bookstore, behind Gimbel's on Ninth Street, where I would select a book from the outdoor sheds in the alley.

I chose a Bobbsey Twins book that first Saturday. It cost a nickel. It was written by somebody named Laura Lee Hope.

After a while, I graduated to Tom Swift books, which cost seven cents. They were written by Victor Appleton. Tom Swift was a boy inventor. In *Tom Swift and His Electric Rifle*, he invented an electrically powered rifle that could shoot farther and straighter than any other rifle on earth.

The Windsor Hotel was a theatrical hotel. It catered to traveling players. In the course of our Saturday visits, Pop introduced me to Singer's Midgets, with whom he played pinochle and who would go on to international fame as the Munchkins in *The Wizard of Oz*; Billy "Cheese 'n' Crackers" Hagen, a burlesque comedian; Spike Howard, a strongman who broke chains across his chest; and Robert Wadlow, the world's tallest man. It is also likely that I was chucked under the chin by a number of burlesque queens.

After a couple of months of Saturdays, our trips to the Windsor Hotel abruptly ceased. Aunt Dot, my mother's youngest sister, would be taking over the Saturday duty. We were going to

**SCHOOL DAYS: STAN**

move from Frankford Avenue to Tacony, a far northern district of Philadelphia. Tacony was like another country. It was vast and undeveloped.

Our house at 7163 Marsden Street had two stories, a basement, and a garage at the rear that opened onto a driveway that served all the houses in the 7100 block. We moved to Tacony when I was in the middle of third grade. Miss McKinney, my new teacher at Edwin C. Forrest Elementary School, was everything a good teacher should be: pretty, warm, and kind. In class we learned about all manner of things. But our real lives were lived in the schoolyard. The Edwin C. Forrest schoolyard was half pavement and half cinders.

Girls kept to the pavement. They jumped rope, played hopscotch, counted One, Two, Three O'Leary as they bounced a ball, and roamed the yard in small geisha-like groups twittering behind their fans.

The boys lived on the cinders. They played fistball, buckbuck, and bag football, a brutal game in which a scrunched-up paper bag served as the football.

A regimen of school, homework, and the early darkness of Eastern Standard Time controlled our lives through most of the school year. There was no regimen after school let out. There was just summer—hot, sweltering, shirtless summer. The only cool spot was the back of Mr. Johnson's ice truck. While the burly iceman delivered blocks of ice, we sneaked into the back of his truck and appropriated the shards of ice that lay on the sodden wooden floor.

No pirated pieces of eight were more prized than those pieces of ice.

In the evening we played wallball, stickball, stepball, halfball, and wireball until the sun set and our mothers called us home.

The urchins of Marsden Street were not indolent. There was

money to be made. The summer after third grade brought with it an unprecedented infestation of Japanese beetles. Mr. Senn, whose property extended from Torresdale Avenue to the Marsden Street driveway, had hundreds of feet of trellised climbing roses, which he treasured. He paid a penny a quart for Japanese beetles (with quart milk bottles serving as the standard measure).

Fortunes were made that summer. Fifty quarts of Japanese beetles equaled fifty cents. I can still feel those bronze-brown little creatures wiggling between my thumb and forefinger as I plucked them from Mr. Senn's roses. Sometimes they were so thick you could just brush them into the bottle. I don't recall that any ethical considerations regarding beetles ever crossed my mind. These were hard times. Beetles were my only source of income. I needed the money to feed my new passion: model airplanes.

**SCHOOL DAYS: STAN**

In my wanderings, I discovered a hobby shop on Torresdale Avenue. Its show window was filled with strips, sheets, and blocks of balsa wood, a selection of propellers, glassine envelopes of basswood wheels, packets of bushings and fittings, tubes of glue, and a pyramid of model kits.

But what made me reach into my pocket and squeeze my beetle money was the jewel-like scale models hanging there as if frozen in a dogfight. They took me back to when I first saw the old general's toy soldiers.

SCHOOL DAYS: STAN

Taking my courage and my beetle money in hand, I entered the store. It was dark and tunnel-like after the blaze of day. There was a tall, bespectacled fellow behind the counter.

"Yeah, kid?"

"Those model kits in the window? How much are they?"

"They're from ten dollars to ten cents."

"Ten cents?"

"The Gullow kits are a dime. Have you got a dime?"

"Yes."

"They're over there—take your pick."

There was a stack of boxes.

I picked one and took it to the fellow at the counter.

"Lockheed Orion," he said. "This your first kit?"

I nodded.

"Good choice. Highwing monoplane. Shouldn't give you any trouble."

I gave him ten pennies. They were still warm from my clenched fist.

While the Lockheed Orion didn't give me any trouble, neither was it a great success.

But I was hooked. I fell in love with balsa wood—with its feel, with its smell, with its incredible lightness of being.

I picked more beetles and went back for another kit. This time I chose the Gee Bee Special, Jimmy Doolittle's racer, also known as the Flying Milk Bottle. The result was an improvement on my Lockheed Orion. I parked my two planes in the hangar-like space under the living room sofa.

For my third kit, I chose a Ford trimotor.

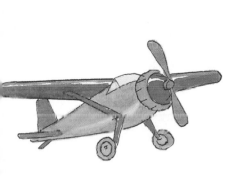
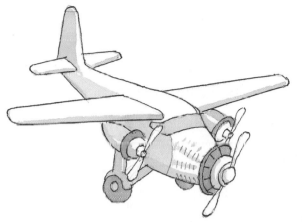
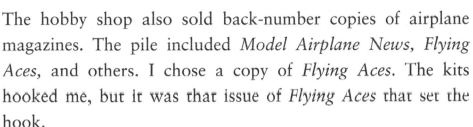

The hobby shop also sold back-number copies of airplane magazines. The pile included *Model Airplane News, Flying Aces,* and others. I chose a copy of *Flying Aces.* The kits hooked me, but it was that issue of *Flying Aces* that set the hook.

I loved *Flying Aces* from cover to cover. Each issue contained an adventure of "G-8 and His Battle Aces," which combined the intrigue of secret intelligence with the high excitement of air combat. For comic relief there were the high jinks of Phineas Carbuncle, an inept airplane mechanic. There were bios of Baron von Richthofen, René Fonck, Eddie Rickenbacker, Ernst Udet, Werner Voss, and other aces. I was so taken with them that I decided I wanted to be a World War I ace when I grew up, which didn't make much sense, but the heart has its reasons.

**SCHOOL DAYS: STAN**

The summer came to an end and I entered fourth grade. If my third-grade teacher, Miss McKinney, was a warm hug, Miss Knowles, my fourth-grade teacher, was a cold shower. On the very first morning, when she called the roll, she took exception to my name. She said there was no such name as Berenstain. The name, as everyone knew, was Bernstein—and *that* was what my name would be, at least in her room. When I raised my hand and protested that Berenstain had always been my name, she silenced me with an icy stare and said she didn't approve of people who changed their names.

Miss Knowles had a problem with another name that morning. When she called the name Gagliardi, she pronounced it gal-YAR-dee, which was the correct Italian pronunciation. Joe protested.

"Hey, my name's Gag-liardi. Not the thing you said." Miss Knowles's icy stare didn't impress Joe. Nor did her lecture to the effect that he should have enough pride in his Italian heritage to pronounce his own name properly. She went on to call the rest of the roll.

Miss Knowles's claim that we were so stupid we didn't know our own names brought Joe and me together. We became school-yard friends. Joe was very tough. He would stand up to fifth and sixth graders. He took it upon himself to teach me how to box. It was probably the only way he knew to be friendly. We would spar open-handed during recess. He was so much faster and more skilled than I that he could have slapped me silly if he'd wanted to. Pop, my fight-fan grandfather, had showed me how to lead with my left. Joe cured me of holding it too high by punching me in the armpit.

Joe never accepted that silent *g* in Gagliardi. He fought Miss Knowles at every roll call. He was of sterner stuff than I. I was "Bernstein" all through fourth grade.

At nine, I was so taken up with such important matters as making model airplanes, drawing, sending in box tops so I could be the first kid on my block to have a genuine Buck Rogers Rocket Gun (it was made of paper), making powerful rubber band guns (with ammunition cut from old inner tubes), walking on oilcans (by stamping empty quart oilcans onto my shoes), and making a general nuisance of myself that I never noticed that my mother was pregnant. My sister, Aline, was born in February of 1932.

Later that year, we moved halfway around the world (as distances are reckoned in Philadelphia), from 7163 Marsden Street in

Eleven-year-old Stan and sister Aline.

**SCHOOL DAYS: STAN**

Tacony to 5410 Chestnut Street in West Philadelphia. Life was different in West Philadelphia. Fifty-second Street, which was two blocks east, was a major business district. Within the five blocks from Market Street to Spruce, there were three five-and-tens, four movie houses, and every kind of store imaginable, including a back-number magazine store next to the State Theater, which offered the biggest and best Saturday matinee.

The four-hour Saturday kiddie matinee was a major institution of the day. I was in line with my ten cents in hand every Saturday. Your dime bought you a seat, the news of the day, a serial with a cliff-hanger ending, an animated cartoon, a cowboy picture, a two-reel comedy, coming attractions, and the main picture. An extra nickel bought you candy from the candy machine.

The options were Green Leaves (leaf-shaped spearmint gumdrops), Nonpareils (sugar-covered chocolate disks), Black Crows (hemispheric licorice gumdrops), Good & Plenty (pink and white sugar-covered licorice bits), and Jujubes, which we pronounced *jujoobs*. They all came in little oblong boxes that, when emptied of candy, whistled when we blew through them during the kissing scenes.

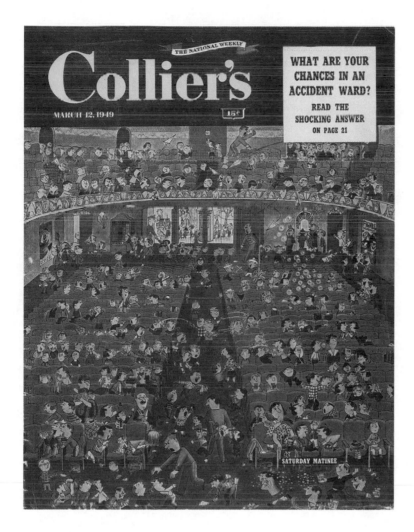

When the Berenstains became cover artists for *Collier's,* they reached back to their childhood Saturday matinee experiences for their first cover.

In addition to being the greatest money's worth on earth, the Saturday matinee was an occasion for mischief (water bombs dropped from the balcony), a scene of crime (tough kids ranged through the audience extorting money from quaking victims), and a place of assignation (boys paired off with girls and would daringly sneak an arm around the back of a girl's seat, sometimes actually touching the girl).

But the most exciting moment was when the film broke—especially if it broke during the serial. Shocked silence would fill the theater when the screen went blank—then fury. Then stomping.

SCHOOL DAYS: STAN

*Stomp, stomp, stomp* would go the feet of two thousand kids. *Stomp, stomp, stomp*—until the very theater shook. Then, just as suddenly, the picture reappeared and Flash Gordon resumed his trip to the planet Mongo in a cardboard spaceship, or Bela Lugosi pressed his toothy attack on the throat of the beauteous maiden, or Bob Steele discovered the bad guy's secret hideaway in the depths of Mystery Mountain.

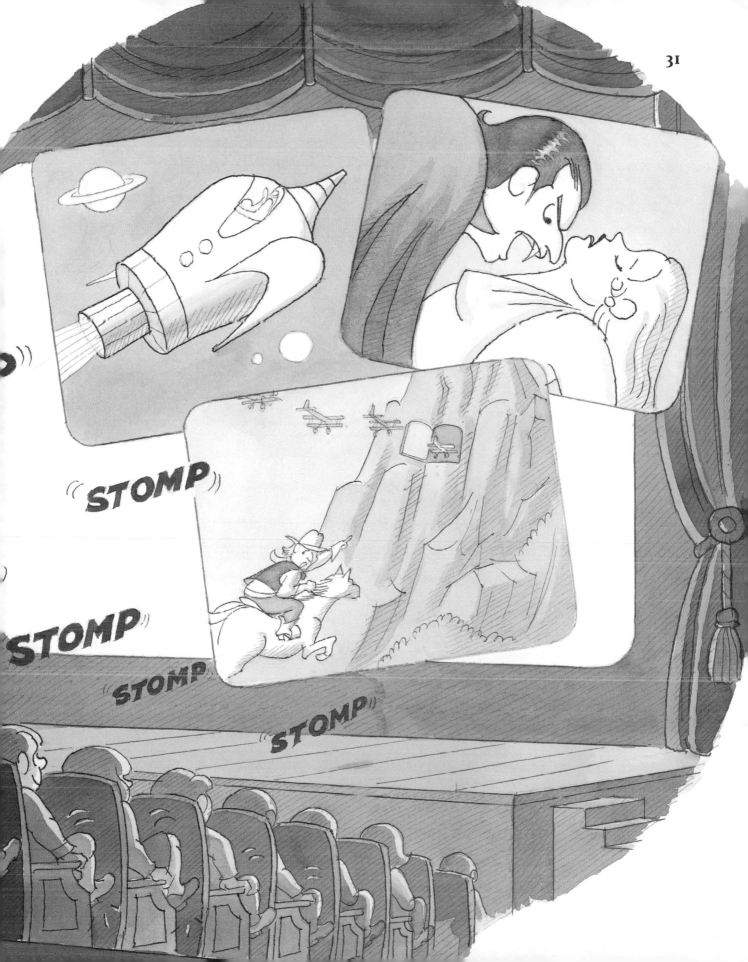

I went to the State Theater every Saturday. I went to the hole-in-the-wall back-number magazine store next door more often. Tip Top Magazines had an inexhaustible supply of airplane magazines. My interest in airplanes had grown. I had graduated from scale models to rubber-band-powered flying models. I had put aside my little-kid notions of what I wanted to be. I was now serious about becoming an airplane pilot.

But I had read enough about flying to know that you had to have perfect vision to become a pilot. I didn't have perfect vision. I was, in fact, virtually blind in one eye.

I first noticed that my left eye didn't work very well when I was learning to wink. When I closed my left eye, I could see the smallest leaf on the farthest tree. But when I closed my right eye, all I could see was a blur.

Being a thoughtful child, given to propounding theories about the nature of the universe (such as my clothes-prop theory about touching the sky), I decided that my condition was like handedness. My right hand worked a lot better than my left hand. I concluded that just as I was right-handed, I was right-eyed. Since according to my reasoning my condition was normal, I saw no reason to tell anybody about it.

I was found out in fifth grade at Samuel P. Huey Elementary School. Motivated principally by the earlier East Coast infantile paralysis scare, the Philadelphia school system instituted a schedule of physical examinations—including an eye examination.

The school doctor sent home a note saying that I had seriously deficient vision in my left eye. The condition was called "amblyopia." I should be examined by a specialist. My parents were astonished.

"Didn't you know you couldn't see out of your left eye?"

"I knew."

"Why didn't you tell us? Why didn't you say something?"

I explained that I had related my condition to handedness—that since I was right-handed, I thought it was perfectly natural to be right-eyed as well.

My mother was stunned, but sympathetic. She smiled through some tears and drew me to her. My father, on the other hand, began hitting himself in the jaw with the side of his hand, a gesture he reserved for moments of great stress.

The eye doctor confirmed that my left eye was, indeed, amblyopic and further that there was nothing that could be done about it. There was a treatment that might have helped if the condition had been caught early—say, at three or four years of age. It involved blocking the good eye with an eye patch so that the bad eye would have to work harder and perhaps improve.

My flying days were over. I got my drawing pad and a pencil. I often drew when I was upset. I went out and sat on the front porch. But I didn't draw anything. I just watched the cars go by.

SCHOOL DAYS: STAN

# SCHOOL DAYS: JAN

ROBERT LOUIS STEVENSON'S POEMS, so evocative of childhood, inspired me all through first grade to master each progressively more difficult phonics lesson so I could go home and "sound out" another one. Still, at the end of first grade, I continued to have trouble with one of them. "SIGH-stem," I sounded out. "What's it mean?"

Mom paused in her ironing as I studied Jessie's beautiful color rendering of a girl reaching for a plump orange in a bowl with several others. "System," she corrected me. "It means an orderly arrangement of things. Having a *system*." Oh. I sort of got it as I read on about the order of things that happen in a child's life (things very similar to my own). Then old Robert Louis disappointed this child with the use of two words meant to rhyme that didn't.

Jan at eight.

1931

> *And every day that I've been good,*
> *I get an orange after food.*

Besides successfully reading my very own first book, it was great to be able to read the Sunday funnies all by myself. My favorites were, one, *Nipper* in the *Philadelphia Ledger,* by Clare Dwiggins—facile pen work featuring a rural setting with a courageous boy character and a tomboyish girl character (just like me, I thought—always playing with the boys). And, two, *Buck Rogers* in the *Philadelphia Bulletin,* whose girlfriend, Wilma Deering, had long, wavy hair flowing from her goggled flying helmet. It was rendered with rows of *C*'s alternating with rows of reversed *C*'s—an artistic revelation to a straight-haired kid

struggling to draw beautiful girls in her sketchbook. Like magic, such a rendition of wavy hair created instant beauty.

As one might expect, going to school in 1930 pretty much ended my tomboy days. Girls had their own sports on gym days and boys had theirs. Girls played with girls at recess and boys played with boys. Ironically, I broke my collarbone play-wrestling with a girl. She got me down on my side, straddled my shoulders, and bounced up and down as if she were on a hobbyhorse. I was taped up with my right arm in a sling and instructions from my doctor not to write for two or three weeks. I was excused from handwriting exercises and from copying arithmetic examples and vocabulary lists from the blackboard. When I sneaked my arm out of the sling for art period, my teacher slipped it back in, saying, "If you can't write, you can't draw," and gave me a storybook to read.

The first time I ever heard of May Day was later that school year. I had heard that "April showers bring May flowers" and I was looking forward to that, but preparations for the first of May at Manoa Elementary School were promising more than just flowers. This was going to be some day—it even looked special on the calendar, which I had newly taken an interest in because of it. Practicing the maypole dance with my classmates and being fitted for one of the German-peasant costumes that a group of mothers were making for the occasion added to my anticipation.

Finally, the day came. Upon awakening, I jumped out of bed and ran into the bathroom, where there was an elevated window beside the toilet with a door handle–type latch that was easy to open. I climbed up on the lid, swung open the window, and leaned out to see what May Day looked like. It looked just like the day before. Hmm. But it was warm and breezy, and hanging out an upstairs window was fun. It afforded you a new and intriguing view of familiar things down below. Directly down below, however,

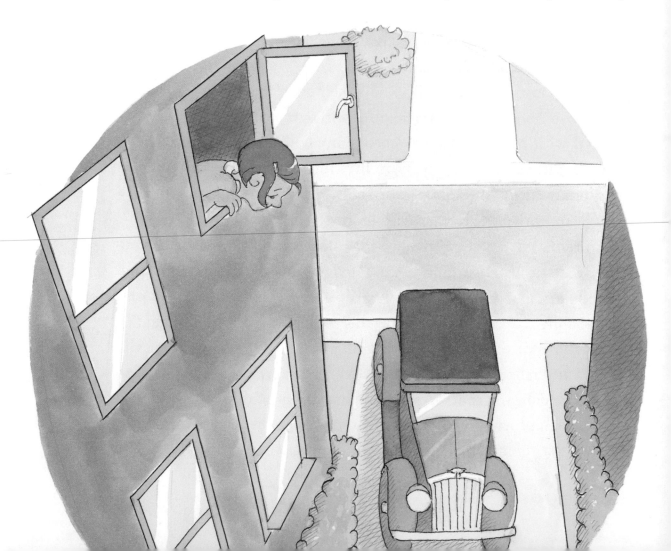

was an unfamiliar thing in our driveway. Quickly dressing in my German-peasant costume, I ran downstairs to the kitchen, where Dad was cooking the oatmeal. "Daddy!" I cried. "Somebody parked his car in our driveway!"

"Oh, he did, did he?" he said, grinning at Mom, who was feeding Charley.

"It's *our* car," Mom said. "We bought it, and Dad drove it home last night." It was a 1923 Dodge sedan, and after oranges and oatmeal, we all piled in and drove to May Day at Manoa Elementary School. Al was dressed in his best knickers, but I never knew what event his class took part in.

Having a car meant Dad didn't have the long walk to the bus stop and the many trolley changes he had to make every morning to get to wherever his job was. It also meant he could take us to a swimming hole in an abandoned quarry on weekends and teach us to swim. Al caught on fast, but I hadn't advanced past the deadman's float and floating on my back before the place was restricted from swimming because of an outbreak of impetigo, a very contagious skin disease.

We didn't get to go swimming again because the next summer, the Great Depression hit the Grant family. Dad's bank closed, he lost his building business, we lost our new house, and we moved back to West Philadelphia. This time we had to jam our furniture into the much smaller living quarters behind and above Granddad's garage and storefront property on Market Street.

The Forty-eighth Street house had been sold, and I suppose that helped to support us through the next three very lean years. Not that we kids were conscious of any deep depression. We were intrigued with our funny new house—and Daddy was home! And was he ever fun! He let us help him renovate the whole place. We hammered nails, brushed paste on wallpaper, and even painted easy places like step risers. He built us another great swing out back under a huge horse chestnut tree, and he painted pictures for the walls—two with pastels and two with oils.

With the place starting to look shipshape, we managed a cheap vacation in Wildwood, New Jersey, sharing a rented house with Aunt Bern, Anne, and Uncle Charles at the end of August. That was the summer of the infantile paralysis epidemic that had developed several years after Franklin Roosevelt was stricken. The Philadelphia schools delayed their opening, and we all stayed on, eating fish and crabs we caught and lots of Jersey corn and tomatoes.

Entering third grade at Henry C. Lea School, where Al had gone to kindergarten and first grade, seemed as easy a transition for me as going back to his old alma mater was for him. It was quite a walk, though, up Forty-eighth Street from Market and down Locust to where the slender four-story red-brick building stood opposite the gigantic West Philadelphia High School. We went up and down stairs a lot at the Lea School, and the kid in front of you usually had a hole in her sock. As a matter of fact, you could sum up the Depression for a kid as always having a hole in one of your socks. A mother had a hard time keeping up with how fast holes sprouted in the cotton lisle socks of the day, especially if she had three kids, a husband, and a granddad to darn socks for—let alone tending to her own silk or rayon stockings. Not many kids got new ones, and after a while our teacher had a brainstorm. In one of our craft classes, she

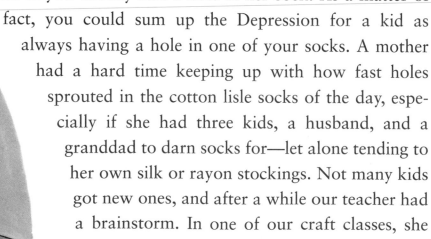

DOWN A SUNNY DIRT ROAD

taught us to darn. We were good at it, too—another instance of healthy young eyes being able to focus close, and nimble young fingers being adept at weaving miniature repairs with a needle and thread on a sock stretched over a wooden egg.

Something this kid wasn't adept at was performing in front of a group.

I could go up to the blackboard and diagram a sentence, execute an arithmetic problem, or draw a picture, but turn around and face the class to speak? Forget it! Faces would blur, a flush would come over my whole body, and whatever words I was supposed to recite would come out shaky.

Imagine my shock and dismay when Mrs. Rhodes asked me to perform in the auditorium for an assembly of the upper grades. Her own shock and dismay showed on her face when I responded that I didn't want to. But she held my hands and buttered me up. "I've been watching you in gym class and you're very athletic," she said. "You're the best in the class in the hop, skip, and run races—and besides, you won't have to say anything."

The buttering up worked and, dressed in an elegant robin costume that my dad fashioned for me with overlapping rows of crepe-paper feathers glued to an old silk slip, I hopped and skipped all around the auditorium while the music teacher sang a song called "Robin Redbreast." We were a hit. The principal wanted an encore, so the music teacher started the song again, and Mrs. Rhodes dragged "shy Jan*eece*" (she never pronounced my name correctly) back for another go. Then the principal took us downstairs to do it for the first and second graders.

Now that everybody in the whole school had seen me as Robin Redbreast, I was relieved to exchange my conspicuous crepe-paper feathers for the comfortable anonymity of an average third grader again. The costume was hung in the teachers' room (purportedly for safety's sake), from which it disappeared before the end of the day, never to be seen again. My disappointment was great—I had hoped to wear it for Halloween later in the year. Al held my hand and pulled me all the way home, bawling my head off.

Apparently, parents can suffer through the hurt and indignity of financial hard times by tending to all the inevitable hurts and indignities their children suffer in the process of just growing up. Having both parents home benefited us kids in other ways, too. We

**SCHOOL DAYS: JAN**

got one-on-one instruction in lots of useful and self-sufficient skills like making model airplanes, rubber band guns, marbles bags and jacks sacks, kites, doll clothes, and paper dolls. We all worked together on giant jigsaw puzzles. We learned how to make "snow-balls" with the ice scraper and flavored them with homemade root beer.

With no jobs to go to, Dad, with Granddad's help, put the car up on blocks to save the tires, and we walked everywhere. We walked to the hockey rink at Forty-sixth and Market, the home of the minor league Philadelphia Ramblers, where they let kids skate on Saturday mornings. We walked to Sunday school at Fifty-first

and Spruce. And we walked to the five-and-ten and to the movies on Fifty-second Street.

I saw my third scary movie, *King Kong,* at the State. Marlyn, a friend from Forty-eighth Street, accompanied me, and Al shepherded us both with instructions from our parents to stay with us. He suggested it might be less scary in the balcony because it was farther from the screen. It seemed farther from the screen at first, but when Kong got loose and stomped all over New York, we felt like the people in the elevated train scene when his giant eye peered in the window. In close-up, he glared at us over the edge of the balcony at *eye level.* Of course, I was a few years older than when I saw my last scary movie, but that just meant I could scream louder.

At the end of fifth grade for me and seventh for Al, lo and behold, the Grant family would move once again to the suburbs. Dad had landed a job as maintenance engineer at the Shipley

School, a private girls' boarding school in Bryn Mawr, and we would live in nearby Rosemont. Our new house was much like the one in Manoa. It was even semi-detached on the same side of its twin—the left.

Public school kids in the suburbs rode buses after completing six grades in their elementary schools. In Rosemont we were picked up by the Radnor Township school bus and driven all the way to Wayne, where the junior and senior high schools were in one large building.

It was invigorating to have a separate art class to go to with an art teacher. Miss Smedley gave us real art problems to solve, too, like cover designs for popular sheet music. Two of my best were watercolor renderings of "Red Sails in the Sunset" and "I'm Putting All My Eggs in One Basket." Georgeann Helms was the other good artist in the class, and we became friends, often teaming up on mural assignments in other classes.

Georgie and I were so close in age that we shared many pre- and post-puberty embarrassments. She grew tall and slim and I grew hips and breasts. Both conditions made us shy with boys. We didn't feel any pressure to remedy the situation, but we did try to learn to dance—she with her sisters in Wayne and I with my brother at the young people's group at our church. Al became a terrific dancer and a popular partner with the girls. But every time a boy ventured to hold me close, I giggled and stepped all over his feet. It was the dead-man's float all over again.

We had admirers, though—of our artwork. We made posters for school dances, sporting events, plays, and concerts. It was a kick seeing kids admiring them in the halls. We played on all the intramural and a couple of the interscholastic girls' sports teams, so we were plenty involved in other rewarding activities. Most of our dancing friends, knowing that high school girls went out on Saturday night dates to the Meadowbrook Ballroom in New Jersey, where many of the big bands got started, aspired to emulate them. Not Janice and Georgie. We aspired to the artist's life. We signed up for peanut gallery tickets to a Saturday night series of youth concerts at the Academy of Music, under the leadership of Leopold Stokowski. The covers of the programs were done by art students. We were inspired both by this and by "Stokie" to continue attending the series through high school.

We also signed up for after-school field trips to the Hedgerow Theater in Moylan, where Wharton Esherick, the woodworker, and Jasper Deeter, the actor, led a community of artists and actors in mounting wonderful productions of the plays of Shakespeare

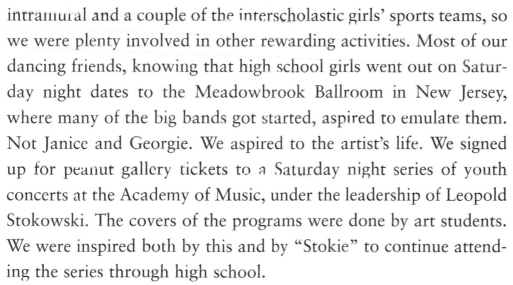

Jan played field hockey as well as other sports throughout her school years.

and Shaw. They all bunked in a nearby farm building and prepared communal meals. *Wow,* we thought, *what a way to live—working and creating with your peers.*

At performances, recordings of classical music were played before the curtain went up and during intermissions, when black coffee was served in tin mugs at a long Esherick table off to the side. We became very fond of Haydn's *Trumpet Concerto,* which seemed perfect for getting into a Shakespeare mood.

## TEEN YEARS: STAN

SOMEWHERE IN THE SEGUE BETWEEN junior and senior high school, I acquired a social grace known as "jitterbugging." Big bands were the driving musical force of the day. You could work up a powerful sweat jitterbugging to Artie Shaw's "Begin the Beguine," Benny Goodman's "Sing, Sing, Sing" (a two-sided number with a long tom-tom solo by Gene Krupa), and Woody Herman's "Woodchoppers' Ball." I did so every Tuesday night in the basement of Beth Am synagogue at Fifty-eighth and Florence in Southwest Philadelphia, to which my family had repaired from our Chestnut Street address.

West Philadelphia High School was a vast brick-and-limestone pile that occupied a full city block and had nearly 5,000 students.

For slow dancing, Beth Am had one of those slowly revolving ballroom lights, which swept the basement with bits of color as we swirled and dipped to the strains of Glenn Miller's "Moonlight Serenade," Tommy Dorsey's "Song of India," and brother Jimmy's "Green Eyes." I can still hear Helen O'Connell singing, "Green eyes, those cool and limpid green eyes . . ."

In high school I came under the influence of Selden Mudge Cary, an art teacher at West Philadelphia High School. West Philly, which was located at Forty-eighth and Locust, was a vast, overflowing three-shift institution that operated from 7:45 in the morning to 4:45 in the afternoon.

Stan at sixteen.

I encountered Cary through the good offices of Arthur De Costa. Arthur, a stout, genial fellow, was reckoned by everyone, even the hypercritical Mr. Cary, as something of a genius. He could draw and paint like a wizard. He knew more about Italian Renaissance painting than Cary, who had a master's degree in the history of art. He also knew music and was the best whistler I'd ever heard.

**DOWN A SUNNY DIRT ROAD**

Arthur first took note of me in Mr. Jarrett's art club. Mr. Jarrett, who was chairman of West Philly's art department, had persuaded his fellow faculty member Mr. Campbell to pose. Mr. Campbell was an English teacher, but his true calling was impersonating Abraham Lincoln, which he did in full regalia at the drop of a stovepipe hat.

Arthur circulated during tests. He admired my drawing of Mr. Campbell, observing that while most of the drawings in the room looked like Lincoln, mine looked like Mr. Campbell *impersonating* Lincoln. From there it was a short step to being inducted into Cary's inner circle.

Though he was an English teacher at West Philly, Mr. Campbell's true calling was impersonating Abraham Lincoln. It was said (only partly in jest) that Mr. Campbell wouldn't be satisfied until he was assassinated.

Though Cary earned his living as an art teacher, he satisfied his soul by writing, producing, and directing the annual spring musical. It was the duty and privilege of the members of his inner circle to help. Seniors Nat Jasper and Bernie Kauffman built the scenery, senior Leon Gonshery notated and arranged the music, and nominal senior Arthur De Costa (his actual grade level was indeterminate, owing to a long-standing inclination to skip classes) designed the scenery, wrote the songs, and served as Cary's production assistant. I, lowly freshman that I was, did as I was told.

The big production of my freshman year was *Go West, Young Man!*, a musical in three acts. It was a "boy meets girl, boy loses girl, boy reacquires girl" fantasy that played on the "Western-ness" of West Philadelphia High School, as, for example, in the opening song:

*When the cactus blooms on Locust Street,*
*diamond stars will hang low.*
*Where the boys all call me Cactus Pete*
*at the big rodeo.*

It was an enormous production with a cast of scores, a ton of scenery, a truckload of rented costumes, a chorus, and even a ballet performed by Mrs. Detweiler's ballet club. I remember Arthur's songs better than he does. Here, for example, is one sung by the juvenile in praise of the object of his affection, a certain Chickie Finkel:

*Oh, I have never seen*
*on any movie screen*
*a looker like my Chickie Finkel.*
*Oh, baby, how her bright eyes twinkle.*
*She's a sight for your sore eyes. . . .*

The ingenue countered as follows:

*I've got my sweetie's picture*
*hanging in my locker.*
*Gee, he's the cutest little thing.*
*He may not be a glamour guy*
*or look like Gable,*
*but he does the homework*
*that I bring. . . .*

The dramaturgy of *Go West, Young Man!* may have been turgid, the production ragged,

the performance uneven, but it was a triumphant success. It played to standing ovations three nights in a row.

Though being a member of Cary's inner circle had its perquisites, it also carried with it certain responsibilities. We had to keep our marks up (except for Arthur, genius having its privileges). We had to show him our monthly report cards. A's and B's were acceptable. C's were sneered at. Anything lower than a C was beyond the pale. We all knew we were subject to being cast into the outer darkness for any of a number of offenses, poor marks being merely the most obvious. Bernie was once threatened with expulsion for putting too much mustard on his sandwich.

Over time, we took to showing up at Cary's tiny Quince Street house, where, with sandpaper and paint scrapers, we spent our Saturdays helping restore the 250-year-old house to its former white-walled, exposed-beam glory. We had free run of Cary's library, his record collec-tion, his kitchen, and his well-stocked mind. The house on Quince Street became a home away from home, a school away from school. Under Cary's mentorship, Arthur, Nat, Bernie, Leon,

Selden Mudge Cary's eighteenth-century house on Quince Street in the heart of old Philadelphia was a home away from home for high schooler Stan and friends

**TEEN YEARS: STAN**

and I became fast friends. Those Saturdays at Cary's tiny little house came to mean a great deal to us. They became an important part of our lives.

Though all good things do not necessarily come to an end, they do, over time, tend to dwindle down. That's what happened to Cary's inner circle.

Mentor stories abound. In so many cases the most unforget-

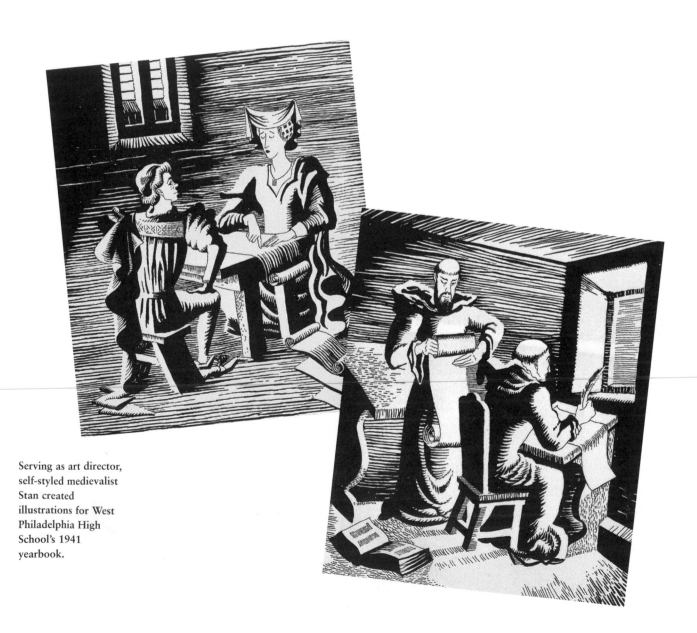

Serving as art director, self-styled medievalist Stan created illustrations for West Philadelphia High School's 1941 yearbook.

table and influential character we've ever met is a teacher or coach who caught us in the yeasty rise of adolescence and helped us find ourselves. Cary would have eschewed, or even scoffed at, the idea that he was anything so lofty as our mentor. But that's what he was. He kept us out of serious trouble. He broadened our horizons. He introduced us to both the joy and the ethic of work. Cary went on to bestow his largesse on other inner circles. But I shall always

TEEN YEARS: STAN

be grateful that I passed through his life. Arthur composed a musical tribute to the house on Quince (to be sung to the opening theme
of Brahms's *Academic Festival Overture*):

> *Quince Street Academy*
> *of the Genteel Arts,*
> *oh, thou shalt ever be*
> *exalted in our hearts.*
> *With spring fading into summertime,*
> *we hear the seasons' knell.*
> *With fall turning into wintertime,*
> *we bid a fond farewell*
> *to Quince Street Academy*
> *of the Genteel Arts.*

If it hadn't been for Cary's badgering, hectoring, and encour-
agement, I would never have won the four-year scholarship that
sent me to the Philadelphia Museum School of Industrial Art,
where I met Jan.

# TEEN YEARS: JAN

IN HIGH SCHOOL, OUR ART TEACHER WAS WAYNE MARTIN, an accomplished painter who welcomed serious art students to his room and tutelage for as many periods as they could schedule. We were a small, industrious group with the freedom to explore projects on our own as long as his supply closet could produce the materials needed.

One year, Mr. Martin was my class's homeroom teacher as well. During one homeroom period a fellow classmate, Mark Shea, asked me to draw his picture. The art closet supplied a large sheet of charcoal paper, and I set to work at an easel in the back of the room. Mark posed with one foot on a stool so he could lean an elbow on his bent knee and rest his chin in his hand. In profile it was an exciting composition, and Mr. Martin urged me to do a painting of it. He provided me with a large square of gessoed Masonite. He demonstrated how to thin out oil paints for painting on gesso and suggested I use a fine brush line for the initial drawing.

I could handle it. Mark Shea never looked so good. Of course, after posing for me through a couple of lunch hours as well as homeroom periods and after school, he was expecting to gain the painting as well as the charcoal drawing. But Mr. Martin had other plans for it first—as did I. He wanted to exhibit it as one of his pieces representing Radnor at the Department of Education's annual "Cultural Olympics" at the Philadelphia Convention Center. And I wanted to exhibit it to my family, especially my dad.

Jan at sixteen.

Radnor High School was a relatively small, highly progressive, much-admired suburban school on Philadelphia's Main Line.

**TEEN YEARS: JAN**

The Cultural Olympics killed two birds with one stone. We all went to the exhibition and saw my painting displayed with the best artwork from all the high schools in Philadelphia and surrounding suburbs. I felt I held my own—even with the excellent work from the sophisticated city schools, like West Philly. (As a matter of fact, one of Stan's paintings represented West Philly. He recalls it was a self-portrait in which he wore the attire of a Picasso rose-period clown.)

I made the varsity field hockey team in my junior year and was elected co-captain with Connie Barrick in my senior year. Sports were an important factor in bridging the perceived gap between the kids in the commercial course of study and those in the college preparatory course. Connie and I were a happy symbol of that bridge. We had been classmates in sixth grade but shared only a couple of classes thereafter—home ec and gym—due to her choice of the commercial track and my desire to prepare for art school. She was a top performer in all her classes and several sports and eventually won a scholarship to Howard University.

Georgie and I would have been competitors if there had been a school art scholarship, so it was probably fortunate that there wasn't. Instead, Mr. Martin had us spend all our senior art periods preparing portfolios to present to two of the area's art schools that had scholarship programs. One of the projects he proposed to be included was going to be difficult to work on in school, however— a series of nude studies. Our friend Esther volunteered to pose at Georgie's house after school if we promised not to show them around. She had early admission to Duke University and was already engaged to her boyfriend.

TEEN YEARS: JAN

Something else that was difficult to work on in school was a job we took on for the yearbook. We were co–art editors and had agreed to render pen-and-ink drawings based on the Tenniel illustrations in *Alice* for practically every page. It was I who tentatively suggested *Alice* for a theme at our first editorial meeting. Georgie liked the idea, but we were both flabbergasted when the editor-in-

Jan proposed an "Alice" theme for Radnor High School's 1941 yearbook, for which she and her fellow artist and art editor, Georgeann Helms, did scores of illustrations. The drawings on these pages are from Jan's Tenniel-inspired hand. Among her faculty caricatures is Mr. Martin with paintbrushes (bottom left).

chief, David Holland, and the literary editor, Henry Fischer, turned out to be big *Alice* fans as well. Not only that, our faculty adviser, Mr. Martin, was another enthusiast.

An operetta, *The Chimes of Normandy,* was the big senior production number that year, with scenery designed by Mr. Martin, built by Mr. Riley's shop class, and painted by Georgie

and me and anybody else we could corral to help part-time. The scenery design was massive, incorporating castle-like structures on either side of the stage as well as within and behind. Two fellow art students who helped out were Tom Yerxa and Inge Probstein. Inge was talented academically as well as artistically, having come from a private school in Berlin the year before. She saw her father get shot in the back by Nazi storm troopers and immigrated to the United States with her mother and brother. She was awarded a scholarship to Agnes Scott College in Decatur, Georgia, after getting a perfect score on her Scholastic Aptitude Test (SAT). Tom was a talented painter who was headed for New York and the Art Students League.

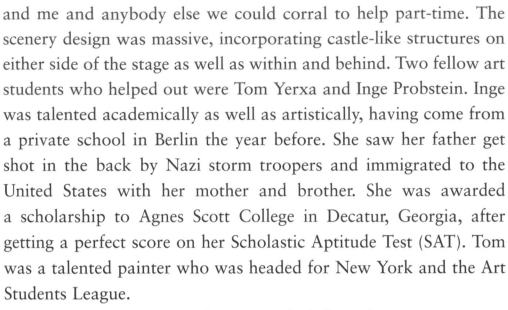

Georgie and I separately followed up on presenting our portfolios to one of the art schools after graduation. We were both offered two-thirds tuition for four years at the Tyler School of Art. Then Georgie's grandmother died and left her widowed mother some money. Mrs. Helms took her girls off on a cruise to Bermuda, and I went off to Ocean City, New Jersey, with Esther. Esther's neighbor owned a small hotel with a popular dining room, where we would be waitresses for the summer.

Jan taking some time off from summer waitressing at an Ocean City hotel at the Jersey shore.

I dutifully sent all my tips home, hoping to contribute significantly to my first-year one-third tuition at Tyler. My folks, however, were worried about the expense and fatigue factors involved in a long daily trek out to the far-northern suburb of Elkins Park, where the school was located. With the Rosemont railroad station so convenient to our house, I would have only one train fare to Broad Street Station in the city, from which I could walk to the Philadelphia Museum School of Industrial Art at Broad and Pine, the other school recommended by Mr. Martin—*and* my dad's old alma mater.

With an interview arranged for when I got home and only a week or two before classes would start, I showed up with my portfolio and my mother to see what in the way of scholarship help was available. I was seen by the dean, who was a well-known watercolor artist. He seemed impressed with my work and announced that I was definitely a candidate for the full-scholarship program, which started in the second year. That's what my mother wanted to hear—and why she came. She opened her handbag, took out a wad of bills, and paid my first-year tuition then and there as the dean signed me up for the class of '45. It was a couple of days after Labor Day in 1941, and classes would start on September 15.

With my portfolio now equipped with charcoal paper, charcoal, sandpaper block, chamois, kneaded eraser, pencil, and thumbtacks, I was ready to go to my first-year drawing class, where I met the boy who was the cure for my shyness.

**TEEN YEARS: JAN**

# STAN MEETS JAN

My first-year drawing teacher at the Philadelphia Museum School of Industrial Art, popularly known as "Industrial," was Miss Sweeny. She was intense, demanding, warm, and motherly. She was a wonderful drawing teacher.

We arrived that first day to the challenge of drawing one of four classical casts: the Phidias *Zeus,* Michelangelo's *Lorenzo,* Houdon's *Voltaire* (terrible to draw), and *The Flayed Man* (terrible

to see). I chose to draw Zeus, despite the fact that he had more curls than Shirley Temple.

Up the line of chairs and low easels was a light-brown-haired, blue-eyed girl who had chosen to draw *The Flayed Man*. She was the only one to do so.

We drew and drew and drew. Except for the scratch of charcoal being sharpened on sandpaper, all was quiet in the whitewashed studio. Drawings by former star students who had gone on to greater things stared down at us. Many were of the same casts we were drawing.

Miss Sweeny patrolled the line of students. She patted backs, squeezed shoulders, and occasionally whispered in ears.

After two hours, she clapped her hands and said, "Now, people, let's stretch our legs and look at what we've done."

With a shuffle of chairs and a wave of stretching, we got up and circulated. The girl up the line was standing back looking at her drawing. A summer tan set off her light brown hair and blue eyes. She was wearing a fuzzy light blue sweater, a gray skirt, and white moccasins.

Her drawing was all bold charcoal strokes and slashes. It was better than any of the drawings Miss Sweeny had hung around the room. Though mine was the second-best in the class, her *Flayed Man* made my *Zeus* seem fussy by comparison.

We had been instructed to write our names in the lower right-hand corner of our drawings. Her drawing said "J. Grant."

Seeing J. Grant herself in full reminded me of how I felt when I first saw those toy soldiers in the Gary Cooper movie and when I first saw those scale models hanging in the hobby shop window, only much, much more so.

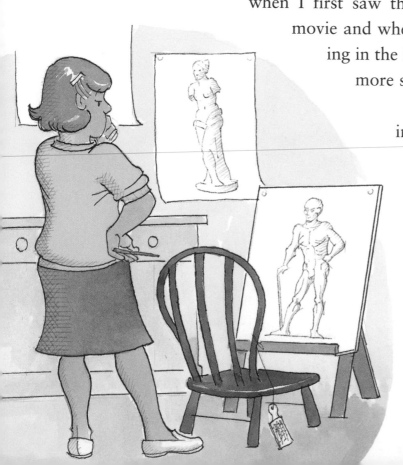

"Hi," I said. "I really like your drawing. How come you chose *The Flayed Man*? I'm Stan. What's the *J.* stand for?"

"Janice. I've done lots of figures and it was the only full figure there." She glanced up the line. "That's a pretty good *Zeus*. How did you manage to do all those curls in two hours?" Her smile came up like thunder 'cross the bay.

**DOWN A SUNNY DIRT ROAD**

She seemed willing to talk. She was from Radnor. She had waitressed at Ocean City for the summer to earn tuition. She envied my four-year Board of Ed scholarship. But she did have a promise of a full scholarship for second year. Did she go to the museum much? Quite a bit. Also the Art Alliance and the Rodin. Did she know about the listening booths at the main branch of the Free Library? No, she didn't. But Dorothy Maynor was going to give a recital at Radnor High in a couple of weeks. Was I interested? *Was I interested?* I was practically jumping out of my skin with interest. Grant, that's a Scottish name. Yes, but she was mostly Irish. She had two Irish grandparents, one Scottish, and one Pennsylvania Dutch. I told her I had a complete set of Jewish grandparents. She didn't seem to mind. She even rewarded me with another smile.

However, when I picked her up for the Dorothy Maynor recital, I got the distinct impression that her mother minded. I got

**STAN MEETS JAN**

no impression of her father whatsoever. He never looked up from his newspaper. Jan told me later that her mother's only comment about me was that she liked the name Stanley . . . for a last name.

I really couldn't blame them, I thought as I walked down County Line Road after the recital. There they were having raised

this perfectly dazzling daughter, and what does she bring home but a skinny, lantern-jawed exotic.

I was headed for the Pennsylvania & Western Railroad, which was the only way back to Southwest Philadelphia. As I walked along the dark road, I became aware of two large dogs that were coming down the hill barking ferociously. They were Saint Bernards. They were bent on protecting the enormous mansion that loomed at the top of the hill by tearing me limb from limb. There was no place to run. There was no fence to hold them back. But—*mirabile dictu*—still barking, they stopped in their tracks at the edge of their lawn. Shaken, I continued on my way. The lights of the Pennsylvania & Western station shone up ahead. *What we do for love,* I thought as I mounted the station steps in a cold sweat.

Jan and I became friends. We took to sitting next to each other in drawing class. On Tuesdays we had nature drawing at the zoo. We often drew the bears at the far end of the zoo. Was our decision prophetic, or did we just want to be alone? We went places and did things. We went to the Museum on the Parkway (the Philadelphia Museum of Art). We touched base at the Rodin. We attended the Annual Exhibition at the Academy (the Pennsylvania Academy of the Fine Arts). We sat in the peanut gallery at the orchestra. We saw Shaw's *Arms and the Man* at the Hedgerow Theater in Moylan. Also *The Devil's Disciple*. Somewhere along the line Jan found out about my secret past as a high school jitterbug.

"I hear you're a jitterbug."

"I have been known to indulge."

"Were you any good?"

"I was the scourge of the synagogue basement."

"The synagogue basement?"

"They had dances there every Tuesday night."

"I don't dance. Do you mind?"

"Not at all. The only reason I learned to jitterbug was that maybe it would help me get a girl. But now I've got one. So I don't have to do it anymore."

"That's right," said Jan.

In December of 1941, Pearl Harbor happened. I had registered for the draft at eighteen. I wouldn't be called up until I was nineteen, which would be in September. So I would be able to start my second year at Industrial. My friends at Quince Street Academy were older than I by at least a couple of years. They were already joining up or being called up.

I received notice to report for my physical a couple weeks into my second year. I reported to the Twenty-seventh Street Armory, where a line of about a hundred youths in undershorts and shoes, carrying the rest of their clothes, snaked among a couple dozen examining stations. My poking, squeezing, coughing examination proceeded apace until I reached the eye station, where a sergeant covered my left eye and directed me to read the smallest line of letters I could make out on a standard eye chart. I read the bottom line.

"Thirty-twenty," said the sergeant.

"Is that good?" I asked.

"Yeah," said the sergeant. "That means you can see at three hundred feet what you're supposed to be able to see at two hundred feet."

He covered my right eye and gave me the same instructions.

"I can't see any of the letters."

"Whaddya mean, you can't see any of the letters?" said the sergeant.

"Just what I said. I can't see any of the letters."

"Oh, Major!" said the sergeant. "This guy says he can't see any of the letters with his left eye. His right eye is thirty-twenty."

The major sat down directly in front of me and looked into my left eye with a little blue light. "Uh-huh, uh-huh—mark him amblyopic, Sergeant." He spelled it. "Have you ever been treated for this, son? You know, with an eye patch?"

"No, sir," I said. I spared him my brilliant handedness theory.

"Sergeant, I want you to see something. Son, look off into the distance." I looked off into the distance. "See how that eye wanders to the left? That's usually a sign of amblyopia. The term means 'wandering eye.'"

*Great,* I thought. *I'm not only a skinny, lantern-jawed exotic, I'm walleyed in one eye to boot.*

I received my induction notice in early November. I was to

**STAN MEETS JAN**

report to the main lobby of Thirtieth Street Station, where I would be sworn in before proceeding by train to Indiantown Gap Induction Center.

The day arrived. I said good-bye to my mom, dad, and sister. I took the Fifty-eighth Street trolley, transferred onto the el at Sixty-second Street and Market, got off at Broad, and walked up Broad to Industrial. I climbed the front steps, perhaps for the last time, and fetched Jan, and we headed back to Thirtieth Street Station.

The main lobby of Thirtieth Street Station in Philadelphia is one of America's great spaces. Vast and gloomy, it was not yet the home of Walter Hancock's soaring sculpture of the Angel of Death supporting a dying soldier (remember the high shot of the little Amish boy looking up at the great winged war memorial in the movie *Witness?*). There would be many thousands of casualties before the war ended. Some, almost inevitably, were in the crowd being checked off by a sergeant with a clipboard.

But I wasn't worried about the future or even thinking about it much. I was more grasshopper than ant. Except for a general notion that I wanted to draw and paint and a steely determination not to let Jan get away, I really didn't think about the future.

I had more or less what I needed in my little carryall bag. I had a sketchbook, a framed photograph of Jan taken when she was a bridesmaid for her friend Esther Shannon, and some extra socks and a sweater.

"Look, hon," I said. "We could be here for hours. You go back to school. I'll write you as soon as I know where I'll be." We kissed. We hugged. We squeezed hands. I watched her as she walked across the vast lobby and left the station.

"Bernstein, Stanley!" shouted the sergeant.

"Here!" I shouted, raising my hand.

# JAN MEETS STAN

THE BIG FIRST-YEAR CLASS WAS SPLIT INTO TWO SECTIONS. Half the students were assigned Miss Schell for drawing and half were assigned Miss Sweeny. I met Stan in Miss Sweeny's class. First I saw his drawing—a big head of Zeus—on one of the low easels, at which he sat working. The classical plaster cast before him was lit with a single spot off to the side. It was very dramatic and, I thought, much too advanced a challenge for me. Not so for this dark-haired wizard with the intense gaze and expert charcoal technique. I saw Miss Sweeny squeeze his shoulder and whisper in his ear. She then drifted around the room taking stock of her new group. We all had lettered our first initials and last names on our papers. Soon she was behind me, checking my work against the cast in front of me— a full figure of a man showing all the muscle systems without benefit of the covering skin. He stood in a graceful hip-shot pose, and I was really caught up in getting this handsome figure right. Miss Sweeny rubbed my back and whispered in my ear, "You love to draw, don't you, Miss Grant?"

"Oh, yes," I said, turning to look into her warm, smiling brown eyes. She liked eye contact, and we would all soon be working like the devil to be favored with the glint of approval in those attentive eyes.

Later, when we had introduced ourselves, I asked Stan what she had whispered in his ear. "Oh, something about how she knew I'd won

72

a city scholarship and was happy to have me in her class. She's something, isn't she? Likes to look you in the eye." We learned she had studied anatomy with George Bridgman, whose book for art students on drawing the human figure was famous. We both flourished under her structured approach, which interspersed the classical casts with live models, nude and costumed.

Works by Jan.
Below: Charcoal drawing of *Head of Alexander*.
Bottom: Pastel of Nancy Lynn in tutu.
Right: Oil on board, Mr. Hearn.

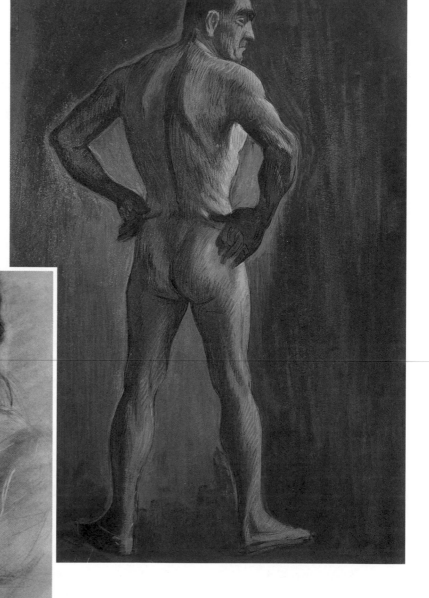

**DOWN A SUNNY DIRT ROAD**

"I wonder what Miss Schell's class is like," I said one day as we passed her door after class. We backed up and ventured in. Some recent drawings of the same casts and models we had done were tacked up. One was signed "G. Helms." I couldn't believe my eyes. In the whirlwind end to my hardworking summer at the shore, followed by my last-minute application to Industrial, Georgie and I hadn't reconnected. I had assumed she was going to Tyler. She probably assumed I couldn't afford either school and, out of consideration, hadn't tried to contact me.

"She's my best friend from high school," I told Stan and his new classical-music-nut buddy, Bill Dugan, when we all finally chanced to meet in the corridor between classes. She and Bill got along, but not nearly as well as Stan and I. We just seemed to need each other's company and support for each other's work. Each new project he completed dazzled me, and I couldn't wait to impress him with mine. Talk about a mutual-admiration society!

Closeness led to physical contact—hugging and kissing (I couldn't get enough of this boy's kisses). Then something happened that I knew instinctively was going to affect the progress of my newly found heaven-on-earth existence. The Japanese Air Force bombed Pearl Harbor. Immediately, President Roosevelt asked Congress to declare war and order the drafting of all young men over eighteen. In another nine months, at age nineteen, Stan would be gone. Practically the whole male population of the school would be gone.

We made hay while the sun shone, however, drawing and painting side by side at school life and costume classes, at zoo nature-study classes, at Rittenhouse Square landscape classes, and at art-museum architecture and composition classes. We had other moments together at concerts, the library, Hedgerow, and Horn & Hardart's Automat, a few blocks from school.

In the summer before he left, we had long train rides to Chester, where we both worked in his father's Army and Navy Store. His whole family worked there, including aunts and uncles. There, I finally met his sister, Aline, who was ten years old and had beautiful long, wavy brown hair. She had a copybook with her filled with drawings of beautiful girls with hair reminiscent of Wilma Deering's, but I think they were more likely inspired by Brenda Starr.

# THE WAR YEARS: STAN

ON MY THIRD DAY AT INDIANTOWN GAP, a sergeant poked his head into the barracks and yelled, "Myclowitz, R., Bernstein, S., Wismer, B.—fall out in the company street in overcoats with all your stuff!" "All your stuff" was code for shipping out.

Why Myclowitz, Bernstein (nee Berenstain), and Wismer? Why us out of the forty men in the barracks? We didn't seem to have anything in common.

Overcoats. That had to mean we were going to a cold place. The Aleutians? Iceland? The North Pole?

Those first days in the Army were so devoid of apparent logic that no rumor, no matter how preposterous, seemed beyond the pale of possibility. In fact, the answer to the question of what we had in common turned out to be almost as preposterous as the speculations as to our destination.

They formed about thirty of us up in the company street, marched us to the post railroad station, and counted us onto the train, where we remained for three days, traveling south.

We spent the three days eating boxed meals, sidetracked as long trains of flatcars carrying tanks and jeeps rumbled by, speculating about our destination, and trying to figure out why we'd been grouped together. There were now two carloads of us.

We didn't find out where we were going until the train pulled to a stop at Fort Bragg, North Carolina. Fort Bragg was vast. It took an hourlong bus ride for us to reach our destination: a nondescript dirt street lined on both sides with two-story barracks. What we saw on the way was anything but nondescript. We saw endless lines of howitzers and self-propelled guns. We saw paratroopers tumbling out of airplanes and sailing through the sky like so many milkweed puffs.

Rumors continued to be rife. We were going into the artillery. We were going to be paratroopers. Didn't you have to volunteer for the paratroopers?

In retrospect, it seems that we might have noticed as we got off the buses and formed up in the company street (there were now about eight hundred of us) that there was a much higher incidence of eyeglasses than might be expected in a large group of draft-age young men. We wouldn't find out until later what we had in common: every man in the battalion was blind in one eye or nearly so.

Our unit would be known thereafter as the "one-eyed battalion." Not officially, of course. Officially, we were designated a "limited-service training unit." As such we could not be sent overseas, where, the reasoning went, our limited vision would represent a hazard to ourselves and others.

It seemed to me that the Army was missing a bet—at least with respect to the fellows in my barracks. They would have made marvelous combatants. Included among my barracks-mates were contingents of one-eyed toughs from South Philly, Northside Chicago, and Manhattan's Hell's Kitchen. They were at each other's throats almost from the beginning, often with fists, occasionally even with knives and bayonets.

The one-eyed battalion did everything the other trainees did. We just didn't do it as long. The only concession to our limited-service status was that our basic training was cut from thirteen weeks to eight weeks.

Our training complete, we wondered what the Army was going to do with us. Apparently, the Army was in a similar quandary.

I had written Jan as soon as I was settled. We exchanged letters throughout my training. I told Jan about my heroic crawl through the muck and mire of the combat course. I drew her a picture of Sergeant Winkowski. I boasted of achieving marksman status at the rifle range. I told her about Maggie's drawers, the big red flag the target crew waved when you missed everything. Jan told me about Miss Hall, her second-year anatomy teacher, who cackled wildly, "Look at the awful drawing that girl did!" It wasn't Jan's, of course. Her anatomy drawings were impeccable.

The principal school news was that Industrial was rapidly losing its male students to the war. Phil Wishnefsky, Russell Hoban, and Bill Dugan had gone into the Army. John Underwood had joined the Merchant Marine.

**THE WAR YEARS: STAN**

With time heavy on our hands, friction broke out in the restive barracks. I pacified the likes of Matterasso, Coelho, and Bowditch by drawing pictures of them to send home to their mothers or girlfriends.

One morning after breakfast, Sergeant Winkowski came to the barracks on an unusual mission. An artist was wanted. My barracks-mates immediately identified me as such. I was to report to Sergeant Borsani at the mess hall on the double. I grabbed my sketchbook and a couple of drawing pencils and headed down the company street. The mess hall was a long, starkly utilitarian Quonset-style building. Its only decoration was the crossed-cannons artillery insignia painted over the front door.

I walked down the center aisle to the counter between the dining area and the kitchen. I knew better than to enter the kitchen area without permission. Sergeant Borsani was busy remonstrating with his cooks.

"Er, Sergeant Borsani," I called.

"Yeah?"

"Sergeant Winkowski said you wanted—"

"You the artist?" He came over to the counter. "Ain't you kinda young?"

"Art student really, Sarge. I brought my sketchbook." I pushed it across the counter. He leafed through it.

"That's pretty good of the water tower. Hey, that's Winkowski!" It was a quick sketch I'd done from memory.

"Maybe you'd do one of me sometime?"

"Anytime, Sarge."

"Okay, come with me." Whatever the job was, I had it.

I followed him through the kitchen and out into the service area behind the mess hall, where stood at least twenty big, smelly empty garbage cans. The sergeant reached into his pocket and took out a folded paper. "It says here what to do."

The paper was a mimeographed order. It said, "All garbage and trash receptacles shall be designated in letters four inches high as containing garbage, bones, paper, metal, or glass." It was signed "Colonel H. R. Melton, adjutant, Headquarters, Fort Bragg, N.C."

"Clean 'em out with hot lye water. Don't get it on your hands. It'll take the skin off. There's a bucket and lye in the shed."

"What about paint and brushes?"

"Inna shed." The sergeant headed back to the mess hall.

"Sergeant!" I cried. "This'll take forever! Just cleaning them out will take me all day! Can you give me any help?"

The sergeant looked at me briefly, then bellowed into the mess hall, "Withers, get your ugly ass out here!" As Sergeant Borsani re-entered the mess hall, Withers emerged. He was a skinny, hungover-looking fellow. He had gotten picked up drunk and AWOL in Fayetteville and was on permanent KP.

The cans were gummy with the filth of ages. It took us the whole morning to clean out five of them with hot lye water.

**THE WAR YEARS: STAN**

Though labeling cans didn't call upon my highest abilities, at least it was in my regular line of work. As I sat alone in the mess hall eating a meatball sandwich from Sergeant Borsani's private refrigerator, trying to think of a way to prolong my tenure at the mess hall, an idea came upon me. I would bestow a mural on Sergeant Borsani's mess hall. The curved Quonset line of the roof formed a panel that separated the kitchen from the mess hall. It cried out for a mural.

Michelangelo had Pope Julius. Velázquez had King Philip of Spain. I would have Sergeant Borsani.

My mural would be a tribute to field artillery. What else? Fort Bragg lived and breathed field artillery. Its crossed-cannons emblem was everywhere.

I opened my sketchbook and went to work on a sketch for my mural. My design consisted of a central medallion with a training scene on one side and a combat scene on the other. The central medallion was to be my *pièce de résistance*.

The only decoration in the mess hall was a framed photograph of Major General Donald Cubbison, Fort Bragg's commanding officer. Just as photos of Roosevelt, Stalin, and Hitler were fixtures throughout their domains, Major General Cubbison's picture graced every mess hall, office, service club, and chapel on the post. A portrait of the general would be the centerpiece of my mural.

I expected resistance from Sergeant Borsani, but he accepted the idea immediately. He was especially favorably impressed with the blatant suck-uppery of my General Cubbison ploy. I'd have to send home for my paints. No, said the sergeant. They held weekend art classes at the service club. He was sure he could get me some paints.

So with a complete set of almost new oil paints from one of the service clubs, special brushes I requested from Jan, and some artillery manuals I borrowed from company headquarters, I commenced my mural.

I worked seven days a week, taking time out only for meatball sandwiches and other delicacies from Sergeant Borsani's private fridge. I can't vouch for the quality of my mess hall mural. It was done a long time ago and there are no photographs of it. But I had a grand time doing it, and I can say with some certainty that it was more fully realized than my earlier mural: the one executed in big red marking crayon on newly papered walls.

It was generally well received. It also elicited a truly remarkable visitation. One morning when the mural was almost completed, there was a cry of "TEN-HUT!" from one of the cooks. I turned and saw a group of officers coming down the center aisle. It included two captains, a major, a bird colonel, and, at their center, a two-star general, whom I immediately recognized as post commander Major General Donald Cubbison.

One of the captains said, "At ease" and came forward to meet a stunned Sergeant Borsani. The general had heard about my mural and had come to see it.

The idea of the two-star general showing up anywhere unannounced, much less at a lowly mess hall, was unheard of.

The captain rejoined the group of officers. He leaned down to hear something the general had to say. The captain came to my station and said, "General Cubbison has instructed me to tell you that this is the finest piece of work he has ever seen done by an enlisted man."

There was one interruption in the course of my triumphal progress to the finest piece of work that General Cubbison had ever seen done by an enlisted man.

One morning when the mural was about half finished, the whole battalion was marched off to take a written test. There was no explanation as to its purpose. It consisted of two sections. The first section posed about fifty algebra problems. Since the mere presence of the letter $x$ in such problems immediately rendered my brain inoperable, I made no attempt to solve them. The second section was a different matter. Each question consisted of a perspective drawing of an irregular solid. The answers were in the form of diagrams that purported to represent the solid as a flattened-out pattern. We were to choose the correct diagram. This section of the test caused considerable consternation among my fellow testees. But since it was a problem of perspective and visualization, it was a piece of cake for me.

I didn't think about the test until three weeks later, when, once again, I was ordered to fall out in the company street with all my stuff. Apparently, I had passed the mysterious test. Once again, I was on a train, this time heading north. Some other trainees and I were going to the University of Maine, where we were to be enrolled in something called the Army Specialized Training Program (ASTP). The program's purpose: to obviate an anticipated shortage of qualified engineering officers, who would be needed to facilitate the invasion of Europe.

Stan in and out of uniform under Army auspices at the University of Maine.
Left: With taller friend.
Right: Standing in front of university gymnasium building.

84

It was a rigorous course for which I was spectacularly unqualified. I couldn't get past the first problem in the physics textbook. It might as well have been written in Sanskrit. It was a crash course, but with a little help from my friends, I managed not to crash.

The University of Maine was a beautiful place and probably still is. Nor was my eight-month stay there uneventful. I went up for a pass during a two-hand-touch football game, came down crooked, and broke my right ankle. I was still in a cast when I woke from a sound sleep one Saturday night and perceived that Hannibal Hall (our dorm was named for Hannibal Hamlin, Lincoln's first vice president and a native of Maine) was on fire.

The remains of Hannibal Hall, the University of Maine's men's dormitory. Drawings done by Stan the morning after he escaped the fire through a window. Two men perished in the fire.

DOWN A SUNNY DIRT ROAD

**DOWN A SUNNY DIRT ROAD**

I was alone in the six-student dorm suite. It didn't take me long to realize that, because of its center-hall construction, there was no escape through the center-hall stairway; it was a mass of flame. Though our suite was on the first floor, it was a flight up from ground level. All I was wearing in bed was the cast. I grabbed my bathrobe and my crutches, opened a window that was about ten feet from the ground, and jumped into a snowbank. It was reasonably soft but very cold.

Two men perished in the fire. It would have been a lot worse had it not been Saturday night. Virtually the whole dorm population was out chasing girls.

After about seven months in which we attended classes, sang

**THE WAR YEARS: STAN**

Stan's first published cartoons appeared in the University of Maine's campus newspaper. *Oglethorpe,* a weekly feature, dealt with the exigencies and embarrassments of the Army Specialized Training Program experience—one in particular being ASTP's Lamp of Learning shoulder patch, which was mocked by combat types.

"The Stein Song," the university's drinking song made famous by crooner alumnus Rudy Vallee, and in my case, contributed cartoons to the campus newspaper (inspired by the cartoon-rich bound copies of *The New Yorker* in the university library), it was decided that engineering officers weren't needed after all, and the Army Specialized Training Program was disbanded. They sent the lot of us to Fort Devens, Massachusetts, where I was reclassified as a trained artilleryman and sent to join the Artillery Regiment of the 106th Lionhead Division, stationed at Camp Atterbury, Indiana.

I had been in the Army long enough to know it would have been futile folly to claim that some sort of mistake had been made.

Lack of artillery training wasn't my only problem. I had over time acquired a condition that can best be described here as the

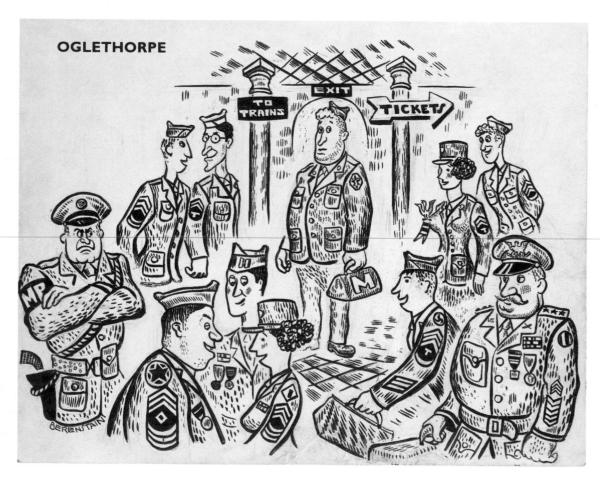

OGLETHORPE

opposite of dysentery. I had no way of knowing it, but I had torn something in the interminable loops and kinks of my innards and was bleeding internally.

I was plugged into a gun crew on my first day and went on field maneuvers on the second day. The crew that mans a 105 howitzer consists of five men and a crew chief. All I would have to do as third man was receive the shell from number four and pass it along to number two, who would shove it into the open breech. Number one would then close and lock the breech and pull the lanyard, whereupon there would be a deafening *BLAM* and the shell would arc about twenty miles downrange and blow up an abandoned farmhouse.

But that's not what happened. When number four passed me the shell, I dropped it point-down on the metal trail of the gun. It was a frozen moment. My crewmates were horrified. The crew chief grabbed me by the collar and called me many names, none of which was "butterfingers." The company sergeant rescued me from the crew chief. "Captain wants to see you," he said as he hustled me up the hill behind the firing line, where Captain Raines was waiting.

"Bernstein?" said the captain.

"Yessir," I said.

I was beginning to feel woozy. The captain, the company headquarters tent, and the woods behind it began to swim.

"Well," he exploded, "what the hell have you got to say for yourself? You could have killed your whole goddamn crew!"

"Well, sir, the shell was heavier than I expected and it just slipped through my fingers."

"Heavier than you expected?" he roared. "Heavier than you expected? Dammit, soldier, your whole purpose in this outfit is handling 105 shells. So don't go telling me—"

**THE WAR YEARS: STAN**

"Begging your pardon, sir, but until today I've never even seen a 105 shell, much less held one."

"Don't try to shit me, Bernstein! I saw your damn papers and I know you had basic at Bragg—and artillery is all they've got at Bragg!"

I did my best to tell him the strange story of the one-eyed battalion and the circuitous glitch-ridden train of events that had gotten me mistakenly shipped into his company. But I was getting weaker and woozier by the minute and made a mumbling hash of it. He sensed something was wrong. He slipped his hand under my helmet. "Boy," he said, "you're burning up with fever. Somebody get this man down to the medical tent! On the double!"

Somebody must have. I vaguely remember being unloaded from an ambulance and gurneyed along the endless corridors of a hospital.

It was days—two? three?—before I emerged from the nether world of surgery. Though I had wisps and patches of dreamlike memories of murmuring nurses and doctors, the glare of OR lights, the rubbery smell of anesthesia, and being asked to count backward from ten, my first reasonably clear memory was of my first visitor. It was Captain Raines.

"How's it going?" he asked.

"Okay, sir, I guess. But I'm not exactly sure where I am or how I got here."

"You're on the asshole ward of Wakeman General Army Hospital. After you dropped that round, you passed out on me. We handed you over to the medics, and they brought you here." He had a barracks bag with him. "I brought your clothes. The doctor says you were bleeding like a stuck pig when they brought you in. They had to do emergency surgery. You had a tear in your rectal wall. He says you'll be in here for at least a couple weeks. That's why I brought your stuff. I can't tell you dates—you know, loose lips sink ships. But I can tell you you're already detached to the hospital." I thanked him for bringing my clothes.

"That's okay. I checked up on that story of yours. Found out it was true. Anyway, good luck, Bernstein."

"You too, sir." I watched as he walked down the ward, fit and trim right down to his polished combat boots.

The 106 shipped out less than a week after my visit from Captain Raines. Months later it was all over the newspapers and the radio that the 106 was the green division that German general Von Rundstedt targeted in the counterattack that was Hitler's last-gasp effort to wrest a negotiated peace from the Allies. It came to be known as the Battle of the Bulge. By all reports, the 106 was decimated.

Indiana was the most bitterly cold place I'd ever been. It was flat as a pancake, and the wind blew down across the Indiana plains uninterrupted from the North Pole. Or so it seemed to Warren Reynolds, Walter Waraksa, and me as we walked from our stations on Colonel Blocker's plastic-surgery service across the utility yard to the mess hall. Wakeman General Army Hospital was all around us.

Stan with buddies at Wakeman General Army Hospital. Left: Stan's oil portrait of Tech Sergeant Warren Reynolds. Right: With Tech Sergeant Walter Waraksa. Both Waraksa and Reynolds were in charge of surgical-dressing stations on Wakeman's plastic-surgery service. Stan was medical artist on the same service.

We tried to hold our breath as we passed the utility plant. Its great brick smokestack was pouring smoke up against the low-hanging sky. Unable to escape, it descended on the yard like a gray shroud. The smell of coal gas was suffocating.

Warren and Walter were commiserating with me. They had each been promoted from T-5 (two stripes with a *T*) to technical sergeant (three stripes above, two below), whereas I was still a lowly T-5. Many things seem strange in retrospect. But for me, my most inexplicable recollection is how I could possibly have been preoccupied with getting another stripe or two, surrounded as I was with the worst horrors of war: the desperately wounded men who were pouring onto Colonel Blocker's plastic-surgery service.

Colonel Blocker had seen me sketching when he toured the ward with Captain Menza, my surgeon. I was doing a portrait sketch of the Mad Russian, an enormous fellow who was a professional wrestler in civilian life. He was really from the Kentucky hills. He had sat in some mustard gas on maneuvers and was in the hospital for a skin graft.

One of Stan's principal jobs as medical artist on Wakeman General Army Hospital's maxillofacial plastic-surgery service was to create "step charts" of the innovative procedures developed by Colonel Truman Blocker, chief of service.

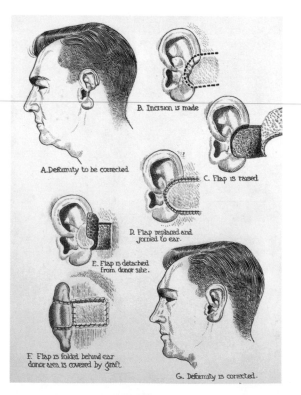

A. Deformity to be corrected

B. Incision is made

C. Flap is raised

D. Flap replaced and joined to ear.

E. Flap is detached from donor site.

F. Flap is folded behind ear donor area is covered by graft.

G. Deformity is corrected.

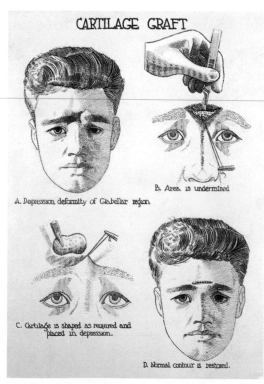

CARTILAGE GRAFT

A. Depression deformity of Glabellar region.

B. Area is undermined

C. Cartilage is shaped as required and placed in depression.

D. Normal contour is restored.

"That's pretty good, son," said the colonel.

"Thank you, sir."

"Are you a queasy type of fellow?"

"Beg your pardon, sir?"

"Can you stand the sight of blood?"

"I don't know, sir. I've never seen any except my own."

"Well, we're going to find out, because I'm founding a maxillofacial center here at Wakeman and you're going to be my medical artist."

Colonel Blocker promoted me from private to T-5 and set me up in a medical art studio on the sunporch of one of his wards. I scrubbed for, observed, and diagrammed as many as eight plastic procedures a day. These included skin grafts, bone grafts, and reconstruction of jaws, eye sockets, noses, and ears. I made step charts of innovative plastic procedures. I made and painted before-and-after moulages (face masks) of representative cases. I painted "glass" eyes, which weren't glass but acrylic, and made and painted prosthetic ears and noses, which were made of soft acrylic.

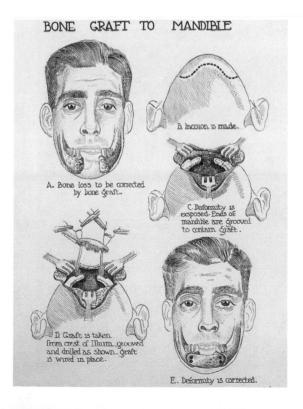

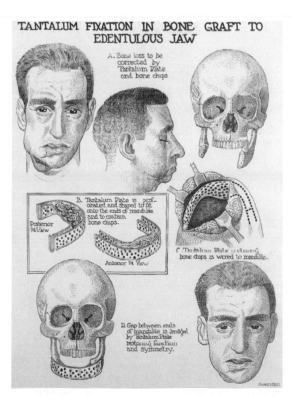

Jan and I exchanged letters two or three times a week throughout my Army service. When school let out for the summer of 1943, she took a course in riveting at Bok Vocational School and got hired on as a "Rosie the Riveter" at Brill's, a former trolley car factory that had a Navy contract to assemble center wing sections for PBY flying boats. We were both saving to get married—I a pittance from my Army pay, Jan a considerable amount from her riveter's salary. Though we were engaged, we were much too bohemian to be bothered with anything so conventional as engagement rings. Jan remedied that omission with her usual verve. She made two elegant rings out of aircraft aluminum and sent me one.

It has been truly said that the course of true love never did run smooth. At some point during the period when I was working on Colonel Blocker's plastic service and Jan was riveting airplanes, we hit an enormous speed bump. Jan's mother—who liked the name Stanley as a *last* name—found a packet of my (admittedly steamy) letters to Jan. She told Jan she suspected my motives and that Jan should inform me that any future mail would be intercepted and

Stan at work in his medical-art studio (note the aircraft-aluminum engagement ring made by Jan).

destroyed. Upon receipt of a tear-stained letter from Jan telling me of her desperate situation, I did what any red-blooded American soldier would have done. I called my mother. I dispatched her to the gate of Brill's, where she located Jan coming off the swing shift and arranged for her to receive my letters at our house on Pentridge Street. Phew!!!

On August 6, 1945, Warren, Walter, and I were walking past detachment headquarters when Top Sergeant Marbury appeared in the doorway looking as if he had big news.

"Hey, you guys!" he yelled. "We just dropped some kind of superbomb on Japan and the war's gonna be over in about twenty minutes!"

On September 2, 1945, the Japanese surrendered to the Allied joint command on the battleship *Missouri*. The mustering-out schedule was based on a system of points awarded for overseas service, decorations and awards, and marital status. Since I had none of the above, I remained in the Army for a number of months. Walter, being married, was the first of our threesome to be discharged. He headed for Shamokin, Pennsylvania, determined not to go back into the mines. Warren was discharged a few weeks later. His old job as a mid-level insurance executive was waiting for him in Newark, New Jersey.

**THE WAR YEARS: STAN**

With my buddies gone, I fell into old habits. For example, I began spending my off-hours in the hospital library, where I discovered a magazine called *The Saturday Review of Literature*. Though it was an interesting magazine in many ways, what struck me about it was that it carried about six cartoons per issue—and they treated of art, music, literature, and history, subjects in which I was interested.

Though I was still more grasshopper than ant, I was beginning to feel it was incumbent on me to at least take a stab at figuring out some way of making a living. Jan, after all, now had two jobs. She was teaching drawing and painting at Industrial and she was doing piecework at the Artgift Company, where she painted floral decorations on trays, wastebaskets, and other giftware.

I went back to my studio and did four cartoons. One showed a quartet of island beauties carrying trays of pineapples on their heads—except that one had a pineapple for a head and was carrying a tray of heads. The second showed an abstract, Picassoesque figure painting a still life. In a reversal of form, the still life was rendered with Vermeer-like realism. The third showed a medieval knight in full armor, armed with sword and shield, confronting a fellow armed with an enormous old-fashioned can opener. The fourth was a parody of the familiar Tabu perfume ad in which a voluptuous female concert pianist is in the passionate embrace of a formally dressed fellow holding a violin. In my version the voluptuous pianist was saying, "Put down that damn fiddle and let's do this thing right."

Returning to the library, I consulted the magazine's masthead, took down the editor's name (it was Norman Cousins), packed my cartoons up with a self-addressed stamped envelope, and sent them off to the magazine's New York address.

About ten days later I received a scrawled note.

"Put down that damn fiddle and let's do this thing right."

Stan received thirty-five dollars for his first professionally published cartoon, a parody of the familiar Tabu perfume ad. It appeared in *The Saturday Review of Literature.*

It said:

> *Dear Corporal Berenstain,*
>    *Buying all four cartoons. Paying 35 dollars per. Your stuff is great! Send more!*
>          *Yours truly,*
>          *Norman Cousins*

Thirty-five dollars per! What a way to make a living! My fortune was made!

I was discharged from the Army on April 1, 1946. I'd been in for three years and three months. Jan and I were married April 13 by Magistrate Bietel in his storefront courtroom on South Broad Street. Present were Jan's parents, my parents, and, at the rear of the empty courtroom, a Philadelphia policeman with a drunk in tow.

**THE WAR YEARS: STAN**

Rarely without his sketchbook, pencil, pen, or brush, Stan was an inveterate sketcher throughout his three-year Army service.

This page, clockwise from top: Waiting room of Indianapolis train station; WAAC with breveted GI; view of Fort Devens's barracks; GI in PX.

Opposite page, clockwise from top: Tough guy; utility building at Fort Devens; Private Gerard Haft rehearsing for officers' concert; band member rehearsing. Center: *Self-Portrait Shaving*, winner of first prize in soldier-art exhibition.

Devens 44

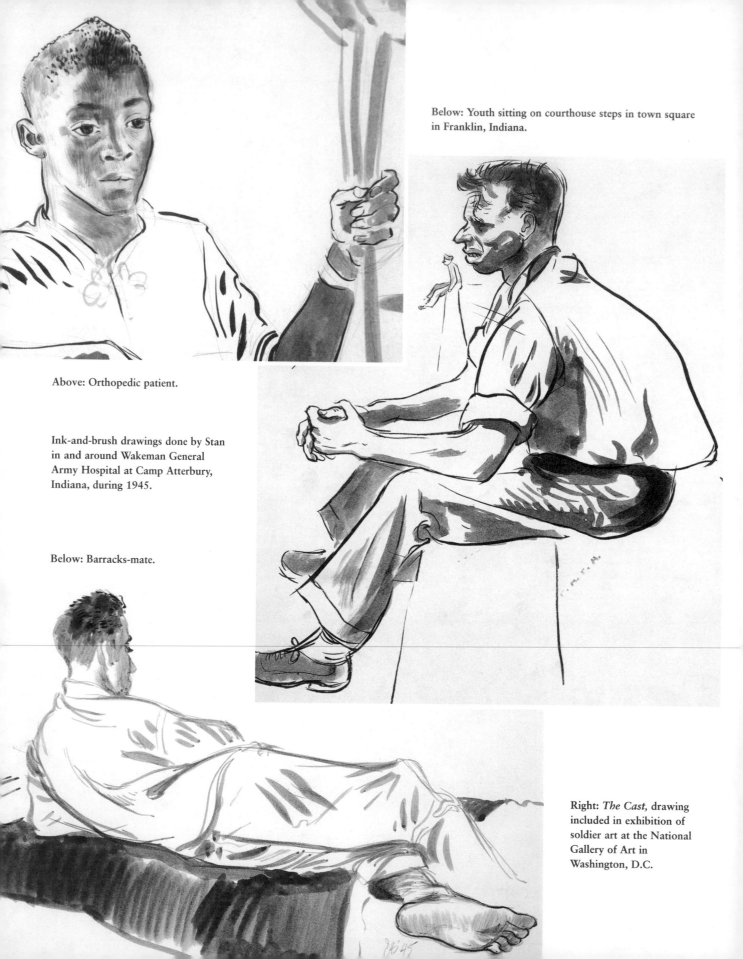

Below: Youth sitting on courthouse steps in town square in Franklin, Indiana.

Above: Orthopedic patient.

Ink-and-brush drawings done by Stan in and around Wakeman General Army Hospital at Camp Atterbury, Indiana, during 1945.

Below: Barracks-mate.

Right: *The Cast*, drawing included in exhibition of soldier art at the National Gallery of Art in Washington, D.C.

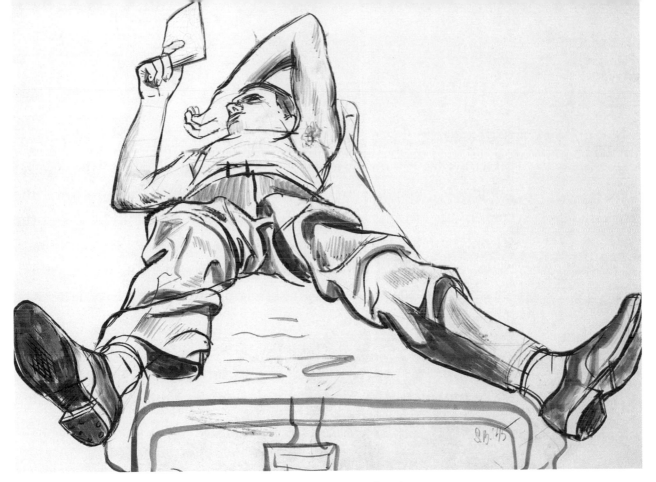

Above: Letter from home.

Water tower, Wakeman General Army Hospital.

# THE WAR YEARS: JAN

WHEN STAN LEFT IN THE MIDDLE OF OUR SECOND YEAR, I relied on his hilarious letters for peace and comfort, and answered them letter for letter. Since the boys who had left before had established the custom of writing to their girlfriends at the school address and the school had hung up a grooved "letter board" to accommodate them, we followed suit. We enjoyed the privacy of it. Besides, there was no way I was going to risk letting any of my love letters be delivered to Rosemont.

At the end of the school term, though, girls were talking about joining the WAVES or the WAACS or doing war work. I was definitely missing the inspiration of working in a full class of talented artists, too, and told Mom and Dad I was going to take a year off from school and earn some money, starting that summer.

I showed up at the U.S. Employment Office on Broad Street with some second-year work I'd done in mechanical-drawing and jewelry classes. I was sent the same day to join a class of young women forming up at Bok Vocational School in South Philadelphia to train to be aircraft riveters. After two weeks of on-the-job training (meaning we were paid), we joined the workforce at Brill's trolley car factory, which had won a Navy contract to assemble center wing sections for PBY flying boats.

Somehow I managed to stop by Industrial every so often to pick up my mail. Then, during one holiday break, there was such a backup of servicemen's mail, it wouldn't fit on the board. The harried office secretary sent it all to the girls' home addresses with a declaration that the school letter board was being dispensed with.

Jan had this photograph taken at Stan's request and sent it to him to replace his prized "bridesmaid" photo, which was lost in the dormitory fire.

**DOWN A SUNNY DIRT ROAD**

I don't know how the other girls made out, but my mom felt it was her maternal duty to open my batch of letters and read them. She didn't think they were so hilarious. She soon had me in angry tears—still the bawler—and I informed Stan in my next letter that we couldn't exchange letters anymore. I simply couldn't handle any tension at home with the demanding work schedule at Brill's.

It was a long, twelve-hour day, six days a week plus an occasional Sunday, with the extra complication of the shift swinging from day to night every two weeks. In other words, the factory was running around the clock, with two groups of riveters taking turns working the night shift. With a train ride, a bus ride, and a trolley ride to and from the factory almost every day, I was lucky to wake up from my exhaustion and make my connections. But Stan's

Jan's riveting class celebrates graduation with a "Rosie the Riveter" party at Frank Palumbo's nightclub in South Philly.

mother had a solution to the letter problem. I could get off the trolley at Fifty-sixth Street, walk the few blocks to Pentridge Street and pick up Stan's letters at *their* house a couple of times a week, walk back, and get the next trolley. She met me coming off the night shift and gave me a key. Problem solved for the time being. Someday I would have to be able to control my emotions and have an understanding with my mother.

It wasn't her fault she was giving me a hard time, I told myself. She was really more worried about Al than me. He had joined the Seabees, the Navy's construction battalions, and was training in the dark waters off Iceland to assemble floating landing docks for the eventual Allied invasion of Europe. We didn't know it then, of course, because his mail was censored. The Seabees maneuvered these vast installations across the choppy English Channel the day before the invasion and attempted to set them up in the dark, undetected. Because of the fierce weather conditions, they were both undetected and unsuccessful. Once assembled, many of the docks broke up in the stormy surf. Many Seabees drowned.

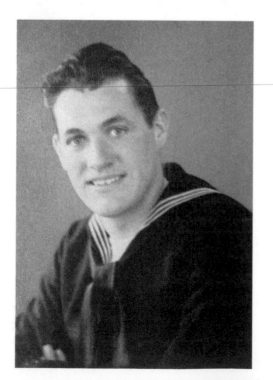

Jan's older brother, Alfred Jr., was in the 28th Seabees, a naval construction battalion that saw action in the Normandy invasion in northern France and in the island-hopping Pacific war.

In the meantime, upon arriving home after a day on the job, I usually crashed on the sofa and dreamed I was still riveting, often shouting, "Buck it up! Buck it up!" in my sleep.

In the 1940s, aircraft was assembled by teams of riveters. Two to a team. One on the outside driving each rivet through lined-up holes with an air gun placed on the head side of the rivet, and one on the inside simultaneously "bucking up" a securing head on the other end with an iron bar. Both could do both and often switched places when the one on the inside cramped up or something. The air gun was a small jackhammer shaped like a handgun, with a long hose coming out of the handle connected to a source of compressed air beneath the factory floor. The iron bar was one of several the "bucker-upper" had that were shaped to fit different rivet locations. I had one partner who preferred being on the inside of the wing assembly all the time in case she dozed off. She had young children in school and a husband in the service and didn't get much sleep during the few hours she was home.

Though the PBY flying boat was the sea and airborne workhorse of the Pacific war, research reveals that the wing sections on which Jan worked were incorporated into planes that were sent to the Soviet Union.

Another partner I had preferred being on the outside, especially when we got to the gas tanks. Big and mature Alice D'Amico was so expert with her air gun, I didn't mind bowing to her advanced age and size status and doing the honors scrambling among the spars and being a contortionist in the gas tanks. We were a good team, though. Our airtight rivets passed inspection after inspection. The only problem I had with working inside the tanks was the smell of the zinc chromate paste that had to go on every rivet to ensure that they were not only airtight but waterproof. When our two tanks (one on each side of the wing section) tested negative for leaks, we got a cheer from the other teams on our jig.

A complication of aircraft riveting in those days was the need to keep the rivets in a frozen condition until they were driven. To soften aluminum, you freeze it. We would pick up the rivets needed from a freezer and keep them in a section of our toolboxes with a chunk of dry ice. We also wore a thin kid glove on the hand that handled the rivets so they wouldn't stick to our fingers.

The factory was equipped with jigs large enough to accommodate our upended center wing sections, which were as big as trolley cars. They were just as long, somewhat taller, but not as roomy inside. I seem to remember there were about ten being worked on, all down the length of the factory

floor. When one was completed, it was hoisted by an overhead horizontal crane that delivered it to the back, where it was sprayed all over with a protective coat of zinc chromate paint. Then, like a giant yellow-green kite, it rose again and slowly sailed forward over the jigs to the open end of the factory, where a huge rack waited for it on the back of a trailer truck.

In about eight months, with the two shifts riveting around the clock, the ten sections were all gone, Brill's contract was fulfilled, and our work was done. We all received pink slips in our final fat pay envelopes. Many of these well-trained Rosies were expecting to get hired on at other Philadelphia-area defense plants. Kellett's in North Philadelphia made autogyros, and Autocar in Ardmore was starting to make helicopters.

**THE WAR YEARS: JAN**

I, however, was expecting to go back to school in six months or so. My fat earnings were socked away in a bank account, so I wasn't concerned about having enough money for art supplies and train fare. I opted for a temporary job as a draftsman at I.T.E. Circuit Breaker Company for lower pay and reasonable hours. Women certainly replaced men very successfully in many factories, and I bet the men they replaced had never worked such long hours. But there was a war on—and those men, now in the service, were working long, hard hours, often in mortal danger.

Keeping your mind off the possibility that any day your boyfriend could be shipped overseas and you wouldn't ever see him again was achieved only by constant work and other exhausting challenges. When I went back to school, I requested and was granted Special Student status. I could take as many advanced drawing and painting classes as I wanted and drop classes that didn't challenge me anymore—interior and fashion design, pottery, jewelry, and ceramics. One of my drawing classes was anatomy, in which we were charged with not only learning the name of every bone in the body and every muscle connected to it but also drawing groups of them without reference.

The intense concentration it took to complete the life-size charcoal renderings of the bas-reliefs of the della Robbia *Madonna and Child* and Parthenon equestrian friezes blotted out all thoughts of war, at least for the many hours of standing before them.

Although Georgie had talked of joining the WAVES because she liked the uniforms, she ran into resistance at home

**DOWN A SUNNY DIRT ROAD**

and was now in her fourth year at Industrial. I had several water-color and costume-drawing classes with her and her friends from Miss Schell's class. Many female models had left to make more money in defense work, and, of course, the young males were being drafted. Students were being pressed into service. Georgie posed once for a head study in pastels. I posed as a Gypsy with a basket of fruit. Margie Boyd posed in a riding habit for a full-figure rendering in watercolor. Barbara Pagett posed in a Victorian silk gown and bonnet for a seated portrait in oils. Lois Kerst posed in a midriff bathing suit for a series of croquis (quick line drawings) in brush and ink. Nancy Lynn posed once in a pink tutu for a pastel study, and another time in a Russian-peasant blouse and cap for a watercolor study.

Jan's sketch of student Helen Cogan posing in painting class.

The last life model to leave was Clarke, an African American youth and everybody's favorite hunk. So we were left with a few old pros who helped out in life classes. One was Mr. Hearn, who was as old as my father and had actually posed as a young man in Dad's night classes, lit by gaslight. Another was Miss Pederman, who came out of retirement with several silvery scar lines on her abdomen, which added interest to her still firm and shapely form.

A painter who had made a name for himself painting aged and dissipated subjects, at the time, was in the back of our minds as we painted Mr. Hearn and Miss Pederman. Indeed, Ivan Le Lorraine Albright's painting of Dorian Gray as an old guy was the shocker in full color at the end of the film *The Picture of Dorian Gray*. He inspired us, but none of us went quite so overboard.

**THE WAR YEARS: JAN**

President Roosevelt died in the spring of 1945, the war in Europe ended a month later, the country heaved a big sigh of relief, my fourth-year friends collected their diplomas, and I interviewed for a camp counselor's job for the summer. Because I had taken some teacher-training courses, I qualified to head the Arts and Crafts Department at Camp Ogontz for girls in the White Mountains of New Hampshire.

I had a cabin of eight-year-olds to supervise as well. They preferred to be called by their nicknames—Cindy, Cissy, Trudi, Ellie, Jackie, and Sari—and they all signed up for arts and crafts. I had an excellent assistant, Dottie Coutts, a teacher from Canada, and we both loved teaching kids how to make things. They made silver slave bracelets, leather moccasins, ceramic pins and pots, beaded necklaces, and stenciled T-shirts. They also drew and painted.

I joined a hiking group of Ogontz girls on my day off and climbed Mount Jefferson. It would have been an interesting trek with proper hiking boots—which I didn't have—but turned out to be even more interesting when my shoes started to fall apart on the descent the next day. I arrived at the bus at the base of the mountain with all my shoe seams split open. Back in the arts and crafts cabin, I stitched them together like moccasins.

While I was away, my girls, avid and experienced campers all, signed our cabin up with another cabin for an "overnight on the

island." This was the first I had heard of an Ogontz end-of-summer tradition. Ogontz Lake was huge and deep and had an island in the middle with a house on it. Only a small cove on the banks of the camp was roped off for swimming and boating. To qualify for an overnight, all participants must be good swimmers and boaters.

Since all the girls and the other counselors signed up as chaperones were qualified, I kept my inadequacies to myself rather than disappoint my girls. I put my life in their small but competent hands, trusted their rowing and paddling skills, and joined in their excitement as they planned the trip. We had a week to prepare. A two-mile walk in the New Hampshire hills to a small country store was de rigueur. We all pitched in for a supply of milk, cocoa, butter, eggs, bacon, pancake mix, maple syrup, chocolate chip cookies (then called Toll House cookies), apples, and marshmallows. The plan was to leave from the mess hall after dinner on our appointed day while it was still light—the boats and canoes all stocked with our food, sleeping bags, and life jackets. Our day came, and to our surprise and exhilaration, it was announced in the mess hall that it was V-J Day. World War II was finally over, and brothers, fathers, and boyfriends who had survived would at long last come marching home.

"There's no place I'd rather be on the night the war is over," commented one of the counselors as our boats made their way to the island to the quiet rhythm of the paddles and oars. The sky was darkening over the lake and the stars were coming out. Now *All's right with the world* was the thought we all shared as we built a campfire in front of the house, toasted marshmallows, drank cocoa, and sang songs well into the wee hours. We slept snug as bugs in our sleeping bags all over the empty house.

I couldn't help thinking how important the summer-camp experience was to these young girls. They were all from privileged homes where most daily chores were done for them. At camp, they made their beds, cleaned their cabins, managed their laundry, helped serve the food, and maintained their personal hygiene all by themselves. Here, on the island, they shared the two bathrooms without complaint and pitched in to cook the breakfast on the two old stoves in the kitchen. One was a four-burner gas range and one was a potbellied wood stove. With three girls and a counselor at the gas range flipping pancakes and scrambling eggs, it fell to me to fry the bacon on the wood stove. None of the others (including the counselors) had ever fried bacon before, and they were all a little intimidated by the pale, greasy condition of the multiple striped slices when the package was opened.

We all agreed it was the best food we had ever eaten, cleaned up the place, and returned to camp in time for mail call and lunch. The counselors had all been receiving mail from servicemen and were now eager to learn when they would be discharged. For some it would be soon and for some not so soon. Stan had filled me in on the hierarchy of the process, and I knew that for him it would be several months.

Back from camp, I learned that Georgie had gotten some illustration work and rented a studio on Pine Street. Margie had gotten a fashion brochure to illustrate and was planning to marry her classmate Harry McNaught as soon as he was discharged. Barbara and Lois were marking time until their boyfriends got home by flower painting at the Artgift Company. More painters were needed, they told me, and I'd be good at it. At the same time, I followed up on an invitation to visit Julius Bloch's studio and see his paintings. Mr. Bloch was my painting teacher at Industrial and had two paintings I was familiar with in the permanent collection of the Philadelphia Museum of Art. He was a wonderful painter of head studies and figure groupings and a popular portrait painter. He let me know he had a job for me if I was interested. The boys were returning to Industrial in great numbers on the GI Bill, and he needed an assistant.

I became not only Mr. Bloch's assistant teaching painting two days a week but also Mr. Merrick's assistant teaching drawing two nights a week. In between, I painted roses, daisies, bluebells, and fruit on trays, wastebaskets, watering cans, and silent butlers at Artgift. I shared an apartment with Barbara at Nineteenth and Locust streets in the city, so the two jobs were manageable. When Mr. Bloch heard why I didn't have much time to continue my oil painting, he said, "Oh well, you know Renoir painted flowers on china for two years."

By now, my parents realized that Stan's and my mutual attraction had lasted through our long separation, and Mom had learned

Stan and Jan's wedding picture: Jan is wearing her second suit, Stan his first.

to like Stanley as a first name. Besides, Al was coming home, Charley had a good job, and they were both planning to marry their girlfriends. Our wedding came first, though—as quickly as we could arrange it after Stan's discharge on April Fools' Day, 1946, and as quickly as he could be fitted for a new suit (his first). I was suited up in a fashionable cocoa brown tunic-length jacket with a longish skirt (my second). It was the thirteenth of April, and ever since then I've considered thirteen a lucky number.

**THE WAR YEARS: JAN**

112

Jan drew and painted industriously
throughout her years at the
Philadelphia Museum School of
Industrial Art.

Right: *Merchant Seaman,* pastel.

Below left: *Victorian Barbara,* oil on board.

Below right: *Man with Jug,* charcoal and Conté.

Left: *Rabbit*, pencil.

Right: *Must Be an Orang*, pencil.

Right: *White-Faced Clown,* watercolor.

Below: *Nancy in Russian Garb,* watercolor.

Below: *Pelican,* pencil.

Right: Suite of
pencil drawings.

Below: *Man with Bottle,* watercolor.

Right: *Man in Blue Shirt,* watercolor.

Left: *Blue Pedestal Bowl with Fruit,* watercolor.

Below: *Charlie,* oil on canvas.

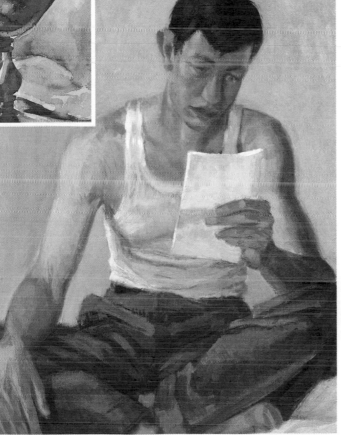

# TEAM BERENSTAIN

WE SET UP HOUSEKEEPING IN A RUN-DOWN, RAMSHACKLE, hot-in-the-summer, cold-in-the-winter, crooked apartment over the Woodland Army and Navy Store at 6141 Woodland Avenue in extreme southwestern Philadelphia. Stan's father had gone into the Army and Navy business for himself at the start of the war. He now had three stores. The Woodland Avenue store was one of them. The first piece of furniture we bought was a drawing table; the second was a bed.

Stan's early notion that doing cartoons for magazines would be a great way of making a living turned out to be a snare and a delusion. We continued to sell occasional cartoons to *The Saturday Review of Literature,* but we had no success in selling to "the majors." The major magazines that used cartoons were *The Saturday Evening Post, Collier's, This Week* (a Sunday supplement), *Ladies' Home Journal, Woman's Home Companion,* and others. There was also *The New Yorker,* of course. It was far and away the most prestigious cartoon market. Regular appearances in *The New Yorker* could lead to fame, rich advertising commissions, and book publication. But we achieved no appearances in *The New Yorker,* regular or otherwise, nor in any other major, for that matter.

Views of the back porch and from the back porch at 6141 Woodland Avenue in Southwest Philadelphia, a very tough neighborhood (note the barbed wire).

Not that the wolf was anywhere near our door. Jan was still teaching at Industrial. Stan was studying painting at the Pennsylvania Academy of the Fine Arts on the GI Bill. But we were strongly attracted to cartooning. It was something we could do together. We'd been apart for more than three years. And together was where we wanted to be.

But try as we would, we couldn't break into the majors. Working together, one of us on one side of the drawing table and one on the other, we cranked out twelve to fifteen cartoons a week and sent them to a succession of magazines—the highest-paying first, the second highest-paying next, the third highest-paying next, etc., until at the tail end of the submission schedule, we sent them dog-eared and tired to the likes of the *Journal of the American Legion* and *Farm Journal*. We had as many as nine batches of cartoons in the mail at any given time. Week after week after week, we'd send them out, and week after week after week, they'd come back rejected. And every week we studied the cartoons in *The Saturday Evening Post* and *Collier's* and tried to figure out what we were doing wrong. After much solemn, self-serving consideration, we concluded that we weren't doing *anything* wrong. It was the magazines that were wrong. Not only were our cartoons wonderfully funny, they were drawn with such zest that we could come to no other conclusion but that there was something rotten in the world of magazines. They were corrupt. You had to be an insider to get published. They were shot through with nepotism. All the cartoons published in *The Saturday Evening Post, Collier's,* and other magazines were the work of the editors' relatives and cronies.

But paranoia is a state of mind that's difficult to sustain. Down deep we knew that the fault was in ourselves, not in the magazines. But what were we doing wrong? We had been submitting batches of cartoons every week for a year to about a dozen magazines *without a single sale*. Our resources of perseverance were exhausted. We decided (at least Stan did) to break through the anonymity of the U.S. Postal Service and seek a face-to-face meeting with the high cockalorum and grand pooh-bah of magazine cartooning, the cartoon editor of *The Saturday Evening Post*. His name was John Bailey. It said so right there on the masthead. The *Post* was located in Philadelphia, just a trolley ride downtown. Indeed, the Curtis Building, the magazine's home, which looked out on Independence Square, was almost as august a Philadelphia institution as Independence Hall itself. When Stan called, John Bailey answered the phone himself. Since Stan was prepared to talk his way past a secretary, he got flustered.

The exchange went something like this:

Stan: "Er, hello, I'm John Bailey."
Bailey: "No, *I'm* John Bailey."
Stan: "What I mean is I'm Stan Berenstain and I've been submitting cartoons—"
Bailey: "Sure, I know your stuff. It's not bad, actually. What's on your mind?"
Stan: "Well, I'd like to come down to see you. Just for a couple of minutes."
Bailey: "Well, I don't know. . . ."
Stan: "I'm just a trolley ride away. . . ."
Bailey: "Okay, then, come on down."

The lobby of the Curtis Building was all echoing marble floors and dark, richly paneled mahogany. Filling the rear wall was an enormous Maxfield Parrish landscape executed in mosaic by Tiffany. The receptionist seemed a mile away across the lobby. Was Mr. Bailey expecting me? Would I please be seated? The elevators weren't as big as the lobby, but they were pretty grand.

John Bailey sat at a large desk. He was lean, fortyish, intense, and slightly bent over. He reached out a bony hand and advised Stan to take care in sitting down—the chair had a loose caster and sometimes collapsed. Gingerly, Stan sat, and gingerly he launched into our yearlong saga of rejection.

Bailey leaned back in his chair and listened, watching closely, his hands clasped behind his head. "Hmm," he observed with some disappointment, "that chair usually collapses." (We found out later from a cartoonist's agent that it really *was* a trick chair and collapsed more often than not.)

"Berenstain, let me ask you a question," he said after listening to our sad story. "Do you ever look at our magazine?"

"Of course. Every cartoon, every week."

"That's surprising. Because every week I get a batch of cartoons from you—and I like your stuff, it's pretty good—and every week your cartoons are about cultural stuff like art, music, history, science. You even had a Shakespeare joke a while back. But *The Saturday Evening Post* isn't about such things. It's a *family* magazine. It's about getting the last bit of toothpaste out of the tube, it's about ladies' stockings hanging on the shower rail, kids stealing cookies out of the cookie jar, taking the dog to the vet, burnt lamb chops. Sure, our readers have heard of Picasso and Freud and Shakespeare, but they're not interested in jokes about them. What they're interested in is jokes about themselves. . . . Well, does that make any sense to you?"

"Yes, it makes a lot of sense. Thanks for letting me come down to see you."

"Okay." He reached over for another handshake. "Hmm, I'm going to have to have somebody check out that chair."

So we set to work doing cartoons about getting the last bit of toothpaste out of the tube, ladies' stockings hanging on the shower

TEAM BERENSTAIN

rail, kids stealing cookies out of the cookie jar, taking the dog to the vet, and burnt lamb chops—*and we began to sell to the majors!*

After failing to sell a single cartoon in our first year of weekly submissions, we proceeded to sell a total of 154 cartoons in our second year. We had *six* cartoons in one issue of *The Saturday Evening Post*—a record.

Note the cartoon in lower right of opposite page. It was the Berenstains' first sale to a major magazine, *Collier's* (frozen foods were still a novelty).

"Don't move! I just want to get a half of an apple I'm saving."

"It's really a crime to take this in black-and-white."

"If anyone calls while I'm gone, I'll be in Lizzy Potash's garage."

"Got anything you want scratched?"

"I don't raise my hand enough."

"Stop eating your heart out. Turn around and take a look."

"Not that towel—the children were lying on it. . . ."

"Life would be a lot pleasanter for me if you'd learn to read those comics to yourself!"

"Wanna hear the ocean?"

"I cut it on some frozen broccoli."

With the initial influence of nostalgia reinforced by the experience of parenthood, the Berenstains became specialists in humor about children.

"Fun for the entire family! Make a whole zoo. It's easy. Simply inflate balloons and follow numbered diagrams . . .
(1) Inflate head A
(2) Inflate balloon B for body and tail
(3) Twist at point A'
(4) Insert meow C at point A'"

"Okay. Come at me."

"How am I supposed to get out of here with you standing there?"

"Make a bunny."

"Why, Peter, what a beautiful landscape." "It's a kangaroo."

"Not bad—for a mouse."

"I'll get it started with a good shove while you run tell Miss McKenna."

"I'll try to explain why you can't play your 'Old MacDonald' record. There's a big, big storm outside and the wind is blowing very, very hard—hear it? . . . Br-r-r!—and somewhere that mean old wind blew a tree down on the electric wires and shut off the electricity and that's why our lights won't light, the toaster won't work, and Mommy can't run the vacuum—Daddy called up the man and he said he's going to fix it real soon. So until it's fixed, nothing that has wires is going to work . . . understand?"

"I wanna hear my 'Old MacDonald' record."

"Dad's on the phone. After he asked to talk to you, I heard him tell somebody, 'Don't be silly. She'll be delighted.'"

Shortly before the turnaround in our magazine cartoon fortunes, we took a job teaching a Saturday morning children's art class at Settlement School, a well-known institution in South Philadelphia. Working with kids, age five to eleven, was more like herding cats than teaching.

But teaching that class took us back. It reminded us of ourselves when we were kids. We began drawing upon our own childhood experiences for cartoon ideas. Kid jokes became our strongest suit.

Our cartoons were so small in print, though—about four by three inches. Not only that, they appeared in the back of the book and were limited to black-and-white. Why couldn't cartoons be big-space features and appear in the front of the book? And color would be fun. With the headlong optimism of youth, we began noodling around with a whole new kind of cartoon. It would be about our new specialty: kids. It would occupy a full page and be in full color. It would show at least a hundred members of the skinned-knee set engaged in every kind of activity known to the schoolyard: kids running, jumping, fighting, wrestling; little girls with holes in their socks strutting past little boys, who were stopping off all the outlets in the bubbler fountain except one, which arced like a geyser onto other little girls swinging on railings, showing their bloomers to other little boys and shouting, "Free show! Free show!" It would be a mad, multitudinous moppet mob scene, the apotheosis of childhood, a modern counterpart of Brueghel's *Children's Games*.

We worked it up and sent it off to Gurney Williams, *Collier's* cartoon editor, who snapped it up and published it under the title *Recess*—in front of the book and in full color. One moppet mob scene led to another. *Recess* was followed by *Freeze,* a tribute to every kind of mischief kids can get into when it snows. *Freeze*

*Recess* was the Berenstains' first full-page, full-color cartoon in *Collier's* in 1948. It recalls the many forms of play and mischief they participated in during their days in Philadelphia-area elementary schools.

was followed by *Gymnasium,* which was followed by *Saturday Matinee.* We could hardly believe it when *Collier's* ran our *Saturday Matinee* as a cover. The response was remarkable. *Saturday Matinee* struck a chord deep in the hearts of everyone who had ever tormented ushers, whistled through candy boxes, and dropped water bombs from the balcony. Thousands of letters poured into *Collier's* editorial offices in New York, paeans of praise were read into the Congressional Record, *Newsweek* came to interview us in our ramshackle apartment over the Woodland Army and Navy Store.

*Saturday Matinee,* our first cover for *Collier's,* elicited the most immediate and overwhelming audience response of all our moppet mob scenes. *Gymnasium,* an interior spread, was a close second. More than fifty years later, hardly a week goes by that we don't receive an inquiry or two seeking to replace a lost or damaged copy. We respond by thanking these phys ed fans for their interest (they frequently ask if we are the same people who do the Berenstain Bears) and advising them that flea markets and back number magazine dealers are their best bets for replacing our tribute to rope burns, muscle pulls, and sweaty underwear.

We were twenty-four. We had gone from being a couple of struggling cartoonists too dumb to come in out of the rain—or at least too dumb to realize that toothpaste and burnt-lamb-chops cartoons were what magazines wanted—to being

The scene and collection depicted in *Art Museum* is an amalgam of the Philadelphia Museum of Art and New York's Metropolitan Museum of Art, two of Stan and Jan's favorite places. The scene approximates the grand hall of the Philadelphia Museum with its large Calder mobile. The Lachaise sculpture is in the Met collection, as are other depicted works. Velázquez's *Court Jester with Glass of Wine* is in neither collection, nor is the portrait of Gurney Williams, *Collier's* humor editor, which we incorporated into the painting.

**DOWN A SUNNY DIRT ROAD**

cover artists for one of the world's leading magazines.

We went on to do more than a dozen covers for *Collier's*. One of them, *Art Museum*, was exhibited at the Metropolitan Museum of Art as part of a world exhibition of cartoon art.

*Penny Arcade*, another Berenstain *Collier's* cover, recalls Stan and Jan's experiences at the penny arcades of yesteryear—at Woodside Park (lost and gone), Willow Grove Park (now a mall), Clementon Lake Park (alive and kicking), and similar enterprises on the boardwalk at Atlantic City and Wildwood, New Jersey. But, of course, they are no longer *penny* arcades. They are now quarter, fifty-cent, dollar, and five-dollar arcades. A couple of grandparents, who shall be nameless, recently spent about a hundred smackers so their grandkids could score enough points to take home about seventy-five cents' worth of key chains.

**TEAM BERENSTAIN**

With the onset of our moppet mob scenes, the support provided by jobs and the GI Bill was no longer necessary. We zoomed into the higher reaches of American cartooning. Our unique status as a husband-and-wife cartoon team helped us take off. It also led to half of our team becoming pregnant. Which, in turn, led to the arrival of Leo, on February 26, 1948.

Following close on Leo's tiny pink heels was a letter from Al Hart, senior editor at a leading New York publisher.

It said:

> *Dear Berenstains,*
>     *I've been enjoying your cartoons.*
> *Have you given any thought to doing a*
> *book? I'd be interested in any book ideas*
> *you might have.*
>
>                     *Sincerely,*
>                     *Al Hart, Jr.*
>                     *Senior Editor*

Stan and Jan's first book, *Berenstains' Baby Book,* grew directly out of their experiences with Leo, their first child.

One of the questions we and other authors are asked most frequently is "Where do you get your ideas?" The answer, in our case, is "from ordinary

everyday experience." Since the letter arrived when we were immersed in the overwhelming everyday experience of coping with a new baby, we hit on the idea of doing a book about the overwhelming everyday experience of coping with a new baby.

Despite the presence of the word "senior" in his title, Al Hart turned out to be a delightful young former Marine officer recently returned from the Pacific war.

Editor Hart liked the idea. There were lots of books of expert advice on child rearing. *Berenstains' Baby Book* would bring up the rear with the inexpert advice of two harried, Pablum-smeared young parents.

It was a slim volume consisting principally of text but with black-and-white cartoon illustrations. No one was more surprised than we at the success of our baby book, unless it was Macmillan, our publisher. Hitherto the distinguished publisher of such celebrated authors as Kipling, Koestler, Sean O'Casey, and Nobel Prize winner Rabindranath Tagore, the Bengali poet, Macmillan took its first tentative step into the light, funny book market with *Berenstains' Baby Book.*

As with our cartoons and moppet mob scenes, one book led to another. We wrote and illustrated a succession of books that

SAY! I HAVE A GREAT IDEA – TONIGHT, INSTEAD OF PLAYING HORSEY...

HORSEY! WE GOTTA PLAY HORSEY!

chronicled our own lives as we moved to Elkins Park, a northern suburb of Philadelphia, where our second son, Michael, joined the family. With titles like *Marital Blitz, Lover Boy: The Last Word in Animal Husbandry,* and *Have a Baby, My Wife Just Had a Cigar,* they found an audience of young marrieds very much like ourselves.

But the general-audience magazines like *The Saturday Evening Post* and *Collier's* would soon hit an iceberg called television and—unable to compete with the new mass medium—would, one by one, sink below the surface of popular culture. And they would take the magazine cartoon business with them.

The Berenstains' many original paperbacks about the agonies of everyday family life were popular during the 1960s and 1970s. They can still be found at flea markets, on eBay, and occasionally in the top of closets of summer rentals.

Fortunately for us, the more specialized magazines not only survived but thrived. We created *It's All in the Family*, a kind of print sitcom for *McCall's*, a leading women's magazine. It occupied a full page and consisted of seven captioned cartoons that told a story. It proved to be popular and ran for many years until a new editor, who thought cartoons were beneath the dignity of an important women's magazine, took over and canceled our feature. But like Eliza leaping from one ice floe to another, we landed at *Good Housekeeping*, where our feature ran for many more years.

Speaking of sitcoms, our *It's All in the Family* started more than a decade before *All in the Family*, of "lovable bigot" fame, was introduced on television. We resented what we considered was the appropriation of our title, nor did we think that bigots were ever very lovable.

*It's All in the Family,* the Berenstains' cartoon feature, ran in *McCall's* and *Good Housekeeping* from 1956 to 1990. Several collections were published in book form.

**Avoid uncaging your pet until it is reasonably well finger-trained, or you may have difficulty getting him back into his cage.**

**Budgie will enjoy a finger-ride back to his cozy cage after a prolonged period of flying about the room.**

**Bits of wood will give him pleasure and provide good exercise for his strong little bill.**

**A well-cared-for Budgie is an endless source of delight. There are cases on record of parakeets living as long as twenty years.**

What with our *McCall's* feature, our books, a greeting-card stint for Hallmark, and our being commissioned to do a series of ads for a leading children's vitamin product (which paid for our little house in the suburbs), we were more than keeping body and soul together. Given the freelance nature of our work, however, we were looking at an uncertain future.

But there was a strange, restless family of bears lurking somewhere in the backs of our minds. Soon they would sweep down on us, push everything else off our drawing tables and writing desks, and take us over, lock, stock, and honey pot.

DOWN A SUNNY DIRT ROAD

# WE MEET THE BEARS— AND THEY ARE US

WE WERE SETTLED INTO OUR HOUSE IN THE SUBURBS with Leo, age four, Michael, not quite one, and Eugenia Diaz, our newly acquired housekeeper. A few weeks before Christmas, we asked Leo if there was anything he wanted Santa Claus to bring him. Yes, he said. There was a book they had at school (Oak Lane Country Preschool) that he really liked. It was really funny and he would really like it for Christmas. He went on to explain that it was by Dr. Seuss and it was about a guy who went fishing in this little pool. Only it wasn't really little. Underneath, it was really big and it had all the different kinds of fishes in the world in it.

Dr. Seuss? Dr. Seuss? The name rang a bell. Wasn't he the one who did those "Quick, Henry, the Flit!" ads we remembered from our own childhoods? Flit was the dominant bug killer of the day. So much so that the pump-type dispensers in use were called "Flit-guns."

"What's this book called?" asked Stan.

"*McElligot's Pool*," said Leo.

"Well," said often-wrong-but-never-in-doubt Stan, "there really isn't any such name as McElligot. It's probably McElliot." Jan protested that the name of the book might well have been *McElligot's Pool*, just as Leo had said.

The Berenstains raised their two sons, a number of cats, a chipmunk, and a parakeet at their residence in Elkins Park, a Philadelphia suburb.

"No," Stan insisted. "There isn't any such name. Tell you what, son. Why don't you ask the teacher to write the name down? Tell her that you want to ask Santa Claus for it and you don't want to get the name wrong."

When Leo got home from school the next day, he handed Stan a note. It said, "The name of the book is *McElligot's Pool*."

We are asked from time to time whether the Papa and Mama Bear of our books are based on ourselves. We usually decline to answer on the grounds that it may tend to incriminate us.

Dr. Seuss's story of McElligot and his ostensibly tiny pool was both a delight and a revelation. It was rollicking, irreverent, and robust, and it was *funny*. Stan went to New York about once a month on *McCall's* and other cartoon business. Leo's standing order for what he wanted Stan to bring him was "funny books." There were lots of cute, charming, interesting books for children, but except for Dr. Seuss, there were precious few downright laugh-out-loud funny books. We became Dr. Seuss fans. *If I Ran the Circus, If I Ran the Zoo, Thidwick the Big-Hearted Moose,* and others became family favorites.

But more than that, they scratched at an old itch. We had for some time been thinking about doing a children's book, perhaps even two or three. Dr. Seuss scratched that itch.

An early attempt to enter the field of children's books had proved awkward, to say the least. It had happened while we were working with Al Hart on *Baby Makes Four,* a sequel to *Berenstains' Baby Book*. When we mentioned that we were thinking of trying a children's book, Al pointed out that Macmillan was a leading publisher of children's books. He would be happy to arrange a meeting with the editor-in-chief of the division.

If the lobby of the Macmillan building at 60 Fifth Avenue, with its ascending double staircase hung with portraits of Nobel

Prize winners, was imposing, the office of the head of the children's division was downright intimidating. She greeted us from behind a large, well-ordered desk that sat at the rear of an inner-sanctum-like office, hung with original art from the many Caldecott winners she had published.

"Mr. Hart has shown me your work," she said, pointing to a small stack of magazines on her desk. We nodded. "He informs me that you wish to explore the idea of doing books for children. And I understand that you have achieved some success with your magazine and other work." We nodded. "But—and I don't know how to say this except to speak plainly—as nearly as I can tell," she said accusatorily, "you are *cartoonists;* your drawings are *cartoons.*"

"Er, well, yes," said Stan. "You see, we've noticed that young children enjoy cartoons, so it was our thought—"

"Yes. But, Mr. Berenstain," said the lady behind the well-ordered desk in the office hung with exquisite Caldecott art, "as I'm sure you and Mrs. Berenstain know, *children like many things that aren't good for them. . . .*"

We wouldn't have been surprised if she had pulled a lever that tripped a trapdoor and sent us screaming down a chute that delivered us into the sewer under Fifth Avenue, where former pet baby alligators flushed down New York toilets were waiting to devour us.

That's not what happened. But that's how we felt. What happened was that we beat an ignominious retreat back to Philadelphia.

*But wait!* we thought. *Maybe doing a children's book isn't such a bad idea after all. Dr. Seuss is a cartoonist, and he's doing wonderful books for children.*

We knew from our first noodlings that our book would be about bears—a family of bears. We knew they would live in a tree. We don't know how we knew, but we knew. We knew we'd have three characters: a bluff, overenthusiastic Papa Bear who wore bib

overalls and a plaid shirt and was a little like Stan, a wise Mama Bear who wore a blue dress with white polka dots and a similarly polka-dotted dust cap and was very like Jan, and a bright, lively little cub who was a lot like Leo.

Michael, not yet one, didn't make the cut.

It took us about two months to write and illustrate the manuscript of our children's book. During that period, two things happened that governed the fate of both the manuscript and its authors. First, a group of editors with whom we were working decided we needed an agent. Their reason: too many legal questions were arising in the course of our helter-skelter cartooning/writing career. Did the "next book" clause in our contract with Macmillan, our hardback publisher, cover original paperbacks? Did we own the book rights to our *McCall's* cartoons or did *McCall's*? Was the "greeting books" project we were working on with Bantam in conflict with our Hallmark arrangement?

While the idea of giving up 10 percent of our earnings to an agent wasn't anathema, it was worrisome to a couple of penny-counting overgrown Depression-era kids. However, given the increasingly complicated job of negotiating contracts, the idea was beginning to sound attractive. But we didn't know anything about

**WE MEET THE BEARS—AND THEY ARE US**

agents. How would we find one? We asked our various editors—Al Hart at Macmillan, Arlene Donovan and Marc Jaffe at Dell, and Knox Burger at Fawcett—for suggestions. They each gave us a list of three or four agents. The names meant nothing to us. But there was the odd circumstance that one name appeared on all of the lists.

"Who is Sterling Lord? How come he's on all the lists?" we asked Arlene Donovan (who went on to become a leading movie producer, most notably, perhaps, of *Places in the Heart,* which won two Academy Awards).

"Well, it sort of makes sense," said Arlene. "What *are* you two? Are you cartoonists who write or are you writers who cartoon? You're neither fish nor fowl. And Sterling is . . . well, *flexible.*"

"Flexible how?" we asked.

"He's open to trying things. Right now, for instance, he's booking Jack Kerouac into coffeehouses for poetry readings."

"Oh," we said.

The other thing that happened was *The Cat in the Hat,* Dr. Seuss's epoch-making response to the "Why Johnny can't read" controversy that was sweeping the country. In seventy-two pages of rhymed, limited-vocabulary text, Dr. Seuss changed the way children learn to read in America. The book was so successful that it led to the development of Beginner Books, a revolutionary new line of easy-to-read children's books. Beginner Books was a new division of Random House. Its trademark (and battle cry) was "I can read it all by myself," and its president and editor-in-chief was Theodor Seuss Geisel, otherwise known as Dr. Seuss.

Beginner Books sounded like a good destination for our own children's book. Our would-be Beginner Book was called *Freddy Bear's Spanking*. It told the story of Freddy Bear, who, having misbehaved, attempts to negotiate himself out of a spanking by proposing a series of alternative punishments. After much negotiation with Mama and Papa Bear, he says, "Oh, the heck with it. Let's go ahead with the spanking."

Did the particular nature of Freddy Bear's misbehavior— marking up the tree house walls—hark back to the spanking Stan received for muralizing those newly papered walls?

Probably.

"Is there anything you'd like me to do for starters?" asked Sterling at our first meeting. When we told him about our grand plan for *Freddy Bear's Spanking*, he said, "Fine. I'll give Phyllis a call."

"Who's Phyllis?" we asked.

"Phyllis is Bennett's wife," he explained to the two hicks from Philadelphia. "She's publisher at Beginner Books."

We did know that Bennett Cerf was chairman and co-founder of Random House. We watched him guess occupations every Sunday night as a panelist on *What's My Line?*

We sent Sterling the Freddy Bear manuscript. A couple days later he called and said he'd had a nice lunch with Phyllis. She loved our work in *McCall's* and was sending a contract over by messenger.

Wow! Whoosh! So that's how it was done! You got yourself an agent who was on a first-name, let's-have-lunch basis with Phyllis Cerf and just like that, abracadabra, presto chango, a contract was sent over by messenger.

It was easier than falling off a log. Unfortunately, it *was* the same log we'd fallen off of when Stan sold the first cartoons he'd ever done to Norman Cousins, of *The Saturday Review of Literature*.

**WE MEET THE BEARS—AND THEY ARE US**

# WE MEET THE CAT

ABOUT TWO WEEKS AFTER RETURNING THE SIGNED CONTRACT, we were summoned to New York for a meeting with the editorial board of Beginner Books. The board consisted of Ted (Dr. Seuss); Helen Palmer, Ted's wife and a longtime children's author in her own right; and Phyllis Cerf, wife of the chairman and co-founder of Random House.

We packed about five of Leo's Dr. Seuss books to be autographed, took the "Pennsy" up to New York, and cabbed over to Random House's headquarters on Madison Avenue. Random House occupied half of a turn-of-the-century mansion (the other half was occupied by the Archdiocese of New York).

A stylish receptionist seated at an elegant antique table instructed us to take the elevator to the fourth floor, where we would shift to a second elevator that would take us to the sixth floor. We weren't to worry about the construction that was going on. They were still working on that part of the building. She hadn't been up there, but she understood that there were signs. "Just follow the signs."

The first elevator was rickety; the second was rickety and

crotchety. We managed to extricate ourselves from its cagelike confines and climb out onto the sixth floor, which was, indeed, under construction. Hand-painted signs, clearly from the hand of the Cat himself, directed us to a newly carpentered stair-case. The first said, "etaoinshrdlu" (which we found out later was the automatic sequence linotype opera-tors used to fill out blank lines). The second said, "This way to Dr. Schmerecase."

"Hi, Berenstains! Come on up," said a tall figure silhouetted in the doorway at the top of the stairs. It was Ted.

Though Ted didn't wear a big red-and-white-striped top hat like the Cat in the Hat, he shared many characteristics with his feline alter ego. Like the Cat, he could be charming, courtly, congenial, and delightful to be with; also like the Cat, he could be demanding, dismissive, and downright difficult. After many of our early meetings with Ted, we would head for home spent, drained, and exhausted, but also exhilarated, excited, and challenged. We would climb onto the train, fall into a seat, and just sit and stare. The train wouldn't be out of the tunnel before Jan would say, "I wonder what Ted thinks of us."

After a bit more staring, Stan would say, "You know, I don't think he thinks about us at all. I think all he thinks about is the work."

That's what Ted was about: *the work*. Every aspect of it: the title, the endpapers, the title page, the meter (he could spot a faulty iamb in your pentameter from a mile away), the rhyme (he was death on convenience rhymes), the type, the paper, the words (every single one), and the pictures (every single one).

Our first meeting began with introductions and pleasantries: Would we like coffee or tea? This was the old Villard Mansion, they explained, and these were the butler's quarters, so they had all the comforts of home. Leo's books were autographed. We compared notes on our war experiences. Captain Geisel had worked on Army training films in Hollywood. Major Frank Capra had been his boss. Stan told about being a medical artist. But Jan got the most points for having been an aircraft riveter.

A slightly disquieting sense of déjà vu hung over the exchange of pleasantries. No wonder. We were literally surrounded by *Freddy Bear's Spanking*. It was plastered all over the walls—

thumbtacked in sequence to large corkboards mounted on three walls of the small room.

"It's called storyboarding," explained Ted. "It's a movie technique. I learned it from Frank Capra. It really lets you get a sense of how the story's working." If it was good enough for Frank Capra, it was good enough for us. Capra was merely the director of some of the best movies ever made, including *It Happened One Night* and *Mr. Deeds Goes to Town*.

"But," said Ted, "before we get into the internal workings of the story, Phyllis and Helen and I want to talk a little bit about these bears of yours."

Internal workings? What internal workings? It's just a funny book about these bears who live in a tree and wear overalls and polka-dot dresses.

"We like your bears. We think they're fun," he continued. "We like the idea of a family."

"And we love your drawings," said Helen.

Hooray for Helen.

"But we need to know more about them. Who are these bears? What are they about? Why do they live in a tree? What does Papa do for a living? What kind of pipe tobacco does he smoke?"

Ted smoked. We didn't. There was no way Papa Bear was going to smoke.

"As I said, we like the idea of a family," Ted went on. "But just what sort of family is it? What roles do they play?"

Roles? What roles *can* they play? They're *bears*.

"I'm concerned about Mama," said Phyllis. "She doesn't really have much to do in the story. She just sort of stands around."

We hadn't thought about it, but it was true. Mama was there, but Papa and Small Bear were the stars.

"True," said Ted. "But I really don't have a problem with that."

It became clear early on that anything Ted didn't have a problem with wasn't going to be a problem. It also became clear as we worked with Ted (we eventually did seventeen books with him) that although he accepted certain broad, general ideas about story construction—that a story needed a beginning, a middle, and an end, for example—he wasn't an editor in any conventional sense of the term. Indeed, he was often dismissive of conventional ideas about story construction. Ted sometimes saw solutions where others saw problems. That was the case with Phyllis's comment about Mama not having much of a role in our story.

"I don't have a problem with Mama being a spear carrier," said Ted. "As a matter of fact, I see the father-and-son relationship as being the heart of your story. Relationships between fathers and sons are one of the great themes of literature."

What literature? We just wanted to do a funny little book about these crazy bears. But somehow we'd wandered into a symposium on the great themes of literature. It was slowly dawning on us that Ted took these little seventy-two-page, limited-vocabulary, easy-to-read books just as seriously as if he were editing the Great American Novel.

"It seems to me," said Ted, "that you've got something pretty interesting going with Papa and Small Bear. Who do you see in those roles?"

We managed not to say, "Huh?" We asked Ted what he meant.

He replied that there was a saying in the movie business that if you cast your show well, you were more than halfway home. He illustrated his point with a horror story from his own experience. He had done a movie after the war. It was a fantasy called *The 5000 Fingers of Dr. T*. Its two major characters were a ninety-nine-year-old man and an eleven-year-old girl. "I wrote a helluva script and it could have been a helluva movie. They not only changed the girl to a boy, they stuck in Peter Lind Hayes and Mary Healy, two broken-down, middle-aged nightclub comics. It was a disaster!"

He was still steaming with the memory of it.

"So you see what I mean about casting. . . . Okay, who are you casting as Papa? Guy Kibbee? Frank Morgan? William Bendix? And who do you see as Small Bear? Roddy McDowall? Freddy Bartholomew? Mickey Rooney?"

We sensed that Ted was dead serious. We had to come up with an answer. We reached back into our collective memory of favorite

**WE MEET THE CAT**

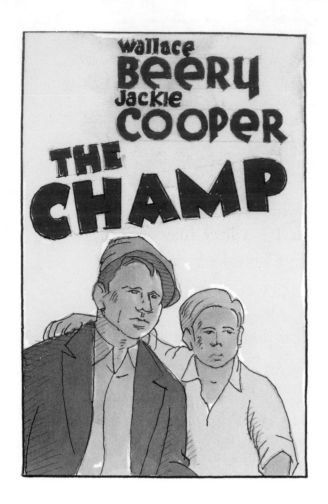

movies and came up with a movie that got us over Ted's casting hump. It was called *The Champ*. It starred Wallace Beery as an overlarge, trouble-prone, loving dad and Jackie Cooper as his bright, resourceful little son.

"Do you remember that old movie *The Champ*?" asked Jan.

"Yeah," said Ted. "With Wallace Beery and Jackie Cooper."

"Well, that's how we see Papa and Small Bear. Papa is Wallace Beery and Small Bear is Jackie Cooper."

Ted pursed his lips and looked off into the distance of the small room.

". . . Yeah. . . . That could work. . . . Okay. Let's get into the guts of your story. There's a helluva lot wrong with it."

We moved to the wall display of *Freddy Bear's Spanking*, where Ted conducted a guided tour of the thousand and one things wrong with our book.

It was too long. It was too complicated. Didn't we realize that these books were supposed to help kids learn to read? Remember the Beginner Book slogan: "I can read it all by myself." We had too many contractions. We had too many female rhymes. We didn't know rhymes had gender. But they did. Female rhymes were those that ended with soft sounds, like "bear/there" and "you/too." Male rhymes were those that ended with hard consonants, like "cat/hat" and "hop/pop." The sentences were much too long—some of them looked like the long, long trail a-winding. "Think short sentences— easy words and short sentences. Think beginning, middle, and end.

As the story stands now, you've got a good beginning and a good end. But your middle needs work—a lot of work. It doesn't really contribute to your story. It's just a lot of pictures. It lacks momentum. It lacks build. It lacks progression. Here's a thought about something you might want to try. I really like the idea of Small Bear trying to negotiate himself out of a spanking. Terrific idea. But as it stands, it's just a series of punishments that Small Bear prefers to the spanking. Now, that's okay as far as it goes. It's a little like when Br'er Rabbit begs Br'er Fox not to throw him into the briar patch because Br'er Rabbit likes the briar patch. But when Small Bear proposes that they punish him by making him go hunt for honey, which is something he likes, you don't go anywhere with it. It just lays here. Why don't you have Papa counter Small Bear's strategy by proposing tougher punishments? Something like . . . oh, I don't know . . . you'll think of something. That way your story can build. You see, these books need to be real page-turners. We've got to keep those kids reading. We've got to keep their little eyeballs glued to the page.

"Well, Berenstains," said Ted, coming up for air, "what do you think so far?"

What did we think? We didn't know *what* to think. We made some noises to the effect that, yeah, we understood what he was getting at. And, yeah, the Br'er Rabbit idea was sort of what we had in mind.

YOU'LL THINK OF SOMETHING.

"Good," said Ted. "Now let's talk about your rhymed verse. Your scansion is pretty good. But again, it's too complicated. And your line lengths are all over the place. They won't look good on the page. Try to even them up. Also, you've got a few interior rhymes. Let's leave interior rhymes to Cole Porter and Ogden Nash. And I've counted at least ten convenience rhymes—"

Phyllis interrupted with a suggestion. "Ted," she said, "since their rhyme doesn't work, why don't the Berenstains just forget about rhyme? Let's have them do the story in prose and then—"

"No," said Ted. "Their rhyme *does* work. I like their rhyme. It's got get-up-and-go. It just needs to be simplified and cleaned up a little."

The meeting was drawing to a close. Helen was taking our book down from the walls. She handed us an envelope containing the manuscript that Ted had just savaged.

But he was all smiles and warmth as he took our hands in his. "Berenstains," he said, "I can't tell you how happy I am to be working with you. I just know we're going to get a wonderful book. And Wallace Beery and Jackie Cooper are perfect casting. . . . Er, how long do you think it'll take for the next draft?"

"Oh, two or three weeks," said whoever managed to recover the power of speech first. But we were thinking, *Maybe never.*

# TED GETS OVERRULED

WE HARDLY SPOKE THE WHOLE WAY HOME. We felt overwhelmed, beat up, abused. No wonder. We'd just gone fifteen rounds with the champ and had been pummeled from pillar to post. Then, after practically knocking us out of the ring, he was all smiles and eager for a rematch. We didn't know if we wanted a rematch. All that stuff about casting and male and female rhymes! *Was he serious?* Besides, we had other fish to fry. We were riding high at *McCall's*. We'd been personally recruited by Joyce C. Hall, chairman and founder of Hallmark, to create a special line of sixteen-page greeting books. *Have a Baby, My Wife Just Had a Cigar* was going into its fifth printing.

We didn't even take the Freddy Bear manuscript out of the envelope. We put it away on a high shelf.

After nursing our wounds and feeling sorry for ourselves for a few days, we took it off the shelf. We had recently added a studio to our house. It was connected by a long corridor. On one side of the corridor were windows; on the other side, a long wall that was perfect for storyboarding. We tacked up the manuscript. After marching up and down the corridor reading and rereading it, we came to the conclusion that not only was Ted serious, his analysis was pretty much on target. Some of the sentences *were* like the long, long trail a-winding. There *were* a lot of convenience rhymes. And the middle of the book *was* kind of shapeless—Ted's idea of dueling punishments might well give the middle more shape.

The term "manuscript" was something of a misnomer. What we had submitted was more properly called a "dummy." A dummy is a rough version of the complete book, with every picture and every block of text in place. A dummy is an enormous amount of work. But we were reluctant to give up on our bear family who lived in the big tree house down a sunny dirt road deep in Bear Country. So we went to work on draft number two, which, over the months, was followed by draft number three and draft number four.

Our modest dream of doing a funny book about a family of bears who lived in a tree was turning into a waking nightmare. We dutifully cranked Ted's recommendations into dummy after dummy and either took them up to New York to present to the editorial board (another misnomer: for all intents and purposes, Ted *was* Beginner Books and Beginner Books was Ted) or sent them to Phyllis, who shipped them to Ted and Helen, who lived in La Jolla, a town in Southern California. The process became progressively manic. It was as if we were on a merry-go-round and couldn't get off. It didn't help that at various points along the way, Ted all but invited us to take the book elsewhere. "Hey, you could probably sell this to Harper just the way it is now." (Harper had launched I Can Read Books, a competing easy-to-read line.)

It's not to say we didn't learn anything in the process. Quite the contrary. We learned a great deal from Ted.

We learned about writing verse. He was a wizard at fixing broken meter and finessing rhyme problems. We learned about advancing the story. "This spread doesn't advance the story," he would say. "Get rid of it." We learned to think cinematically. "You might try a long shot here," he would say, or "Go for an extreme close-up of Papa on this spread," or "You might try a copter shot here." We learned about keeping the reader reading. Each spread had to be more exciting than the one before. Though that was certainly a good idea in principle, the problem was that Ted tended to build excitement with wild Seussian action rather than the homely everyday events that were our stock in trade. Papa's proposed punishments grew wilder and wilder.

As preposterous as it sounds in the telling, we reached a point in the fourth dummy where Papa was pulling giant trees up by the roots and threatening to bash Small Bear with them. That's when Helen and Phyllis called a halt.

"Ted," said Helen, "this is getting crazy. You're turning this into a Dr. Seuss book. That's not what Stan and Jan do. They do warm, funny family stories."

"That's right," said Phyllis. "We've already got a Dr. Seuss. Let's back off and let Stan and Jan be Stan and Jan."

Ted sat back. Some of the air went out of his tires. He looked up at the storyboard where Papa was chasing Small Bear with an enormous tree. "Hey, maybe you're right," he said. "What do you suggest?"

Helen and Phyllis were ready with a suggestion. The honey-hunting sequence had survived all the changes. Why not, they suggested, take that sequence and expand it into a whole book?

That's what we did.

We went home and started from scratch. Our new story told about the Bear family's waking up to an empty honey pot one morning. Papa and Small Bear take the empty pot and set out in search of honey. A bee flies by. Papa and Small Bear "follow that bee and follow that bee and follow that bee to its honey tree." But when they get there, the bees rise up and chase Papa into a pond. On their way home Papa and Small Bear buy some honey at the honey store, which was what Mama wanted them to do in the first place.

We roughed it out and sent it up to Phyllis, who sent it out to Ted and Helen, who thought it was just fine. "Go ahead with the finish," they said.

The fever had broken. The crisis was past. We had our Bears back and all was right in the tree house.

*The Big Honey Hunt* was published in the spring of 1962.

*The Big Honey Hunt,* the Berenstains' first children's book, served as the model for their first half-dozen books about the Bear family. In it, "often wrong but never in doubt" Papa Bear teaches (by bad example) a valuable lesson.

# OFF TO THE RACES

WE TAKE *HONEY HUNT* down from the shelf and look at it from time to time—prompted by a fan letter, or query, or reprint request. When we do so, we find it remarkable for what it wasn't rather than for what it was. One of the principal things it wasn't was well drawn—neither by our present standards nor by the standards of our work at the time. We both were classically trained and had been at the top of our class at Industrial. Jan had taught drawing and painting at Industrial, one of the country's leading art schools. Stan had had a painting juried into the Academy Annual Exhibition, which was recognized as second only to the Carnegie International in prestige and importance, and one of his Army drawings had been included in an exhibition of soldier art at the National Gallery in Washington. So we certainly knew how to draw.

It's not that we don't like the book. We like it very much. And kids like it. They frequently mention it in fan letters as a favorite. It remains in print after almost forty years and is still going strong.

I will get you honey.
I said I would.
But that bee's honey
Was not too good.

27

But when we look at it today, it appears almost as if we had forgotten how to draw. The Bears were drawn with such wild abandon that we wonder what we were thinking. Maybe that's why Ted liked them so. Wild abandon was a Seuss specialty. They were executed in a loosey-goosey pen line and splashy watercolor. Their muzzles shot up like bananas. Black noses perched precariously atop the muzzles. The Bears' tree house was so worm-thin that it wouldn't have accommodated mice, much less a family of bears. As for funny—our bears were on beyond funny. They had toothpick ankles and straw feet. On some pages Papa looked like a haystack wearing overalls. The bee was pretty good and the trees weren't bad. And the drawing actually began to improve toward the end of the book. The honey tree, when Papa and Small Bear finally reached it, was quite a creation. It was a huge, swollen barrel of a tree, filled and dripping with honey and surrounded by hundreds of angry bees, each one saying *b-z-z-z*. We'd never seen anything like it. Nobody else had either.

**DOWN A SUNNY DIRT ROAD**

But *The Big Honey Hunt* rhymed, had short sentences, a strong beat, and simple language, and was *very easy to read*.

So we were off to the races. We were all set to do a series of books about our crazy bears who lived down a sunny dirt road deep in Bear Country.

A few weeks after *Honey Hunt* went into production, Ted called. He and Helen were coming east. He invited us to lunch. We would celebrate the publication of *Honey Hunt* and perhaps discuss what our next book might be. Stan hung up the phone, and we looked at each other. It had been a tough fight, but we had won.

We met Ted and Helen at Random House and walked over to the Park Lane Hotel, where we would be having lunch. Lunch was posh, pleasant, and relaxed. Ted had a bullshot (beef bouillon and vodka), Helen had white wine, and to demonstrate our sophistication, we had Gibsons (martinis with an onion instead of an olive), a drink we had been introduced to by Gurney Williams, our editor at *Collier's*.

With dessert on the way, Ted said, "Well, Berenstains, what do you have in mind for your next book?" What we had in mind, of course, was the next book in a series about our bears.

"Well, Ted," said Stan, "we figure that since we've got these bears all worked out, what we want to do is a whole bear series, and for the next book—"

"Worst thing you could possibly do," said Ted, looking off into the deep space of the elegant hotel dining room. "A series would be a millstone around your necks. Besides, there are already too many bears. Sendak's got some kind of a bear. There's Yogi Bear, the Three Bears, Smokey Bear, the Chicago Bears. No, for your next book you should do something as different from bears as possible."

We were shocked, stunned, catatonic. We remained so through dessert, the taxi ride to the station, and much of the train ride home. After a long mutual silence, Jan turned and said, "Talk to me, hon! Talk to me!"

The advertisement on the front panel of the train car was for Kool mentholated cigarettes. It said, "Smoke Kools!" It featured the Kool Cigarette penguin skating in an arctic setting. As the Pennsy hurtled past Trenton and into the outer reaches of North Philadelphia, the following exchange took place:

> Stan: "I've been looking at that 'Smoke Kools' poster."
> Jan: "Uh-huh."
> Stan: "What do you think about penguins?"
> Jan: "Well, they're certainly different from bears."

Hey, maybe Ted was right. Maybe there *were* too many books about bears. Ted had been around a lot longer than we had. There certainly weren't too many books about penguins. As far as we knew, there weren't any. We'd have the whole penguin market to ourselves.

We'd think further about it in the morning.

# NOTHING EVER HAPPENS AT THE SOUTH POLE

WE AWOKE THE NEXT MORNING WITH A SENSE OF LOSS. We'd had our hearts set on a bear series. We had worked so hard getting to know our bears, cultivating them, bringing them into being. Besides, we were series people. Our *McCall's* feature was a series. Our moppet mob scenes were a series. We were comfortable with series. But we proposed and Ted disposed. And there wasn't a thing we could do about it. It took us a while to get over our disappointment, but we did.

We began thinking about penguins. We began noodling around with a penguin character. We handed penguin sketches back and forth. A character began to appear. He was a cute little guy. He wore a little wool hat and a long red scarf and lived in an igloo. But we needed a story. The South Pole environment wasn't exactly teeming with story possibilities. Nothing much happened at the South Pole. Maybe that was the key to our story—though "nothing happening" was hardly a promising idea. But we thought of something that offered the glimmer of a story. It was an old Popeye cartoon, one that starred Popeye's girlfriend, Olive Oyl. The premise of the cartoon is that Olive Oyl is a sleepwalker. In the cartoon Olive rises from her bed and sleepwalks through a series of hazardous locations: a train yard where she barely misses being run

**NOTHING EVER HAPPENS AT THE SOUTH POLE**

over, a factory where she comes within an inch of being ground up in the machinery, and a construction site where she walks onto a girder being lifted to the highest reaches of a skyscraper. But she is completely oblivious of these events because she is sleepwalking.

It was a good cartoon, but it was missing a significant element: Olive lacked motivation. There was no purpose in her sleepwalking except to provide the framework for an entertaining animated cartoon. Ted was a bug on motivation. Then there was our motivation. We were powerfully motivated to come up with another book. The last thing we wanted was for our Beginner Books relationship to be a one-book stand.

Having kicked off with the best-selling *The Cat in the Hat*, the Beginner Book line was hot. Ted followed the Cat with *Green Eggs and Ham*. P. D. Eastman weighed in with *Are You My Mother?* and *Go, Dog. Go!* Submissions were arriving from unlikely sources. Truman Capote, an important author on the Random House adult list, tried his hand at a Beginner Book. It wasn't surprising that submissions from well-known authors were pouring in. Beginner Books looked so easy. "Put a simple one-hundred-word story together and make big bucks!" seemed the order of the day.

We were determined to retain our place on the Beginner Books assembly line. So there was no shortage of motivation on

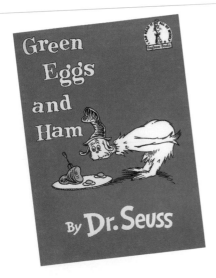

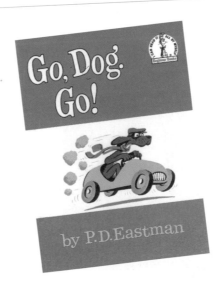

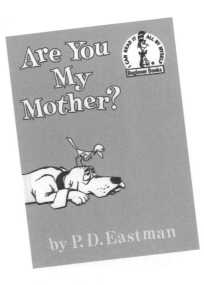

our part. What we had in mind for our little igloo-dwelling penguin was a polar walkabout along the lines of Olive Oyl's sleepwalk. But how to motivate such a walkabout? We hit on the idea of a diary—the kind with lock and key and a pencil on a string. One morning, just such a diary arrives in the igloo (we figured a diary arriving out of nowhere was covered by cartoonist license). Our penguin opens the diary. The first page says, "Walk around the South Pole and write down what happens every day!" Our penguin dutifully embarks on his polar walk, pencil at the ready. Things happen—cataclysmic things: icebergs thrust up through the ice cap, polar bears attack giant walruses, killer whales attack polar bears. *But they all happen behind our penguin, just after he has passed.* So he is completely oblivious of them. (We gave him earmuffs so he wouldn't hear the racket.) He walks all day. He returns to his igloo, opens his diary, and writes, "Nothing ever happens at the South Pole." End of story. That's what we called it: *Nothing Ever Happens at the South Pole.*

We did our penguin book up brown, or to be precisely accurate, we did it up red and blue. Our penguin book not only would *be* different from *Honey Hunt,* it would *look* different. We did the whole thing with one of those blue-at-one-end, red-at-the-other-end pencils that came with kids' pencil cases. Our penguin's hat and scarf and the cover of his diary were red. Everything else in the book was icy blue.

We knew when Ted and Helen would be coming east again. We called Phyllis and, without giving away what the book was about, arranged for a meeting to present it to Ted and company.

The atmosphere in the eagle's aerie–like former butler's quarters was as cordial as ever, but strangely subdued. "Well," said Ted, "let's have a look." He sat at a desk up near the front of the office. Helen and Phyllis weren't crowding around as they usually did.

NOTHING EVER HAPPENS AT THE SOUTH POLE

Helen was busying herself at the rear of the room. And Phyllis had disappeared into the kitchen. We placed the dummy on the desk and hovered nervously as Ted proceeded to go through it. *"Nothing Ever Happens at the South Pole,"* he intoned. "Helluva title. . . . Hmm . . . about a damn penguin . . . cute little bugger. Good idea—the business with the diary. Wonderful drawing. It's really quite beautiful. . . ." But he was only about halfway through it when he looked up. "Berenstains, let me run something past you. An interesting thing has happened. The salesmen have *The Big Honey Hunt* out on the road. And it's going over big. The buyers love it. We've already upped the first printing. So let me ask you. What would you think about doing another bear book next? There's no reason why there couldn't be a whole bear series." The offices were quiet and still. Dust motes sparkled in the sun rays streaming in the high windows. "But I like this penguin book a lot. We'll just put it on the back burner," he added.

"Yeah, sure," said Jan. "I think we could do that."

"Sure, we're game," said Stan.

Ted beamed. He stood up and grasped Stan's hand. Then he gave Jan a big hug. Helen was grinning. Phyllis was bringing a tray of cups of coffee. There were cookies.

Almost forty years later, our penguin book is still on the back burner.

# THE BERENSTAIN BEARS

ONCE IT WAS DECIDED THAT A BEAR SERIES WAS A GOOD IDEA, the editorial process went reasonably smoothly. In *The Bike Lesson,* our second bear book, Papa brings home a two-wheel bike and proceeds to teach Small Bear how to ride it. After each demonstration of bike-riding technique (Papa teaches by bad example), Papa says, "That is what you should not do. / So let that be a lesson to you."

Ted produced the finished book at our second celebratory lunch. The cover looked like it was supposed to. There was Papa riding downhill with Small Bear hanging on for dear life against a background of 90 percent magenta, with the book's title in big yellow letters. But something new had been added. In a dropped-out white box, it said, "ANOTHER ADVENTURE OF THE BERENSTAIN BEARS." We were puzzled. It was very nice. But we didn't quite get it. We asked Ted what it meant.

"You know," he explained, "your bears are a vaudeville troupe like Murgatroyd's Mules and Dugan's Dogs." Though, goodness knows, Ted could be difficult and quirky (and would be again), he was also capable of remarkable acts of generosity. It never would have occurred to us to name the bears after ourselves. After all, we were the Berenstains and our bears were the Bears. Ted's generosity and marketing savvy in eponymizing our bears (*eponymous* [adj.]: giving one's name to a place, tribe, creature, or other entity) were what put our funny bears on the road to becoming what is known in the larger world as a "property." And that wasn't all. He sharpened and

*The Bike Lesson was based on Stan's attempt to teach son Leo to ride a two-wheeler.*

shortened our byline from "Stanley and Janice Berenstain" (which it was on *Honey Hunt*) to "Stan and Jan Berenstain." "Hey, that's what you call each other," he said. "Besides, it rhymes."

So Dr. Seuss not only named our bears, he renamed *us*.

With our snappy new name (we didn't have the nerve to actually put our name in the titles for years) and *The Bike Lesson* under our belts, we really *were* off to the races with our bear series. The books that followed, *The Bears' Picnic, The Bear Scouts, The Bears' Vacation, The Bears' Christmas, The Bear Detectives,* were all variations on the theme established in *Honey Hunt* and *Bike Lesson:* Papa sets out to instruct Small Bear in some aspect of the art of living and ends up badly the worse for wear, with Small Bear expressing his appreciation for the fine lesson Papa has taught him.

Papa spares himself nothing. In his effort to fulfill his responsibility as Small Bear's First Teacher, he goes over a cliff, gets caught in a whirlpool, runs afoul of skunks, porcupines, mosquitoes, crocodiles, and a hay baler, mistakes the open mouth of a whale for an underwater cave, suffers himself to be struck in the seat of the pants by lightning, gets dumped on by a garbage truck, and receives such other punishments as a couple of determined cartoonists could devise.

Hmmm. This cave
is big and wide!
It might be safe
to go inside.

think you should?
Something tells me
it wouldn't be good!

And we spared ourselves nothing in our effort to fulfill the Beginner Books mission: *to help children learn to read*. We used the entire easy-to-read armamentarium to keep those pages turning: easy words, short sentences, word/picture clues, rollicking rhythm, resolute rhyme—not to mention such cartoonist's tools as shameless slapstick and outrageous jokes. All calculated to elicit the proud cry of the Beginner Books trademark: "I can read it all by myself."

Although the editorial/authorial road ahead was now reasonably smooth, we did hit an occasional pothole. The Beginner Book format offered the luxury of full-color endpapers. They were great fun to do. We had a wonderful time drawing every imaginable kind of picnic food for *The Bears' Picnic*'s endpapers: sliced olives with pimento, a wedge of Swiss cheese, pickles, liverwurst, three kinds of pie, and chocolate cake to die for. Ted's response: "Looks like a damn delicatessen. Do something else." We looked at it. Ted was right. It did look like a delicatessen.

There were occasions when we stood on principle and resisted Ted. Consider the case of the length of Papa Bear's finger- and toenails, for example: "Papa's finger- and toenails are too damn long!" pronounced Ted in the course of going through *The Bears' Vacation*. "They make my teeth hurt!"

It was bad news when Ted's teeth hurt. But artistic integrity required us to take a stand. We backed our stand with a letter from a boy who held a contrary opinion. "I really like your books," said the letter. "My favorite character is Papa Bear. His fingernails and toenails are awesome!"

Ted backed off. Kids' opinions had a certain standing with him. Since he and Helen had no children, Ted had little experience with them. It appeared to us that the only child he truly related to was his own inner child—and the child he had been back in Springfield, Massachusetts, where his father had been curator of the Forest Park Zoo.

We, on the other hand, were immersed in children. Not only were they our stock in trade, they were our life experience. We were up to our hips in them—not only our own two boys, but their many friends, who toured our studio virtually every day. We wanted to try something a little different. But Ted was very happy with our Papa-Bear-as-lovable-screwup. The books were proving very popular and by all reports were helping children learn to read. But we still wanted to do something that related to our everyday experience with children. We proposed a story in which Small Bear and some friends find a trunkful of Papa and Mama Bear's old clothes in the attic and have a high old time dressing up. We worked up a cover sketch and an outline. Ted looked at it and shook his head. "Nope," he said. "This is just Norman Rockwell stuff. Kids really don't do that." We knew from experience that it wouldn't have done any good to try to persuade him otherwise.

"Besides," he added, "you've got this Papa Bear thing working. If it ain't broke, don't fix it."

But you never knew with Ted. We would soon get our chance to do something different. Ted was about to spring an entirely new kind of book on us and the world.

# DÉJÀ VU ALL OVER AGAIN

WE CONTINUED TO BE BUSY ON ALL FRONTS. We were still doing our monthly feature in *McCall's,* our paperback cartoon books were still selling, and although our run as *Collier's* cover artists had ended, we were frequently commissioned to create moppet mob scenes for various national advertisers—a disparate group that included the Shell Oil Company, Keds, and Bosco, the maker of the chocolate drink. And, of course, there were the bears.

We were working on the text of *The Bear Scouts,* which would be our fourth bear book, when Ted called from La Jolla. After a quick hello he said, "Can you put Jan on the other phone? I need you both on this." While Jan hurried down the long studio corridor to pick up the house phone, Ted dropped a bombshell. "You guys'll be working directly with me from now on. Phyllis has decided to leave Beginner Books. Bennett is setting her up with her own division." Jan picked up the other phone. "Is that you, Jan? You two are working on the scout thing now, right? Well, I want you to put it aside for now."

He went on to tell us he was starting a whole new line called "Bright and Early Books." It would be much younger than Beginner Books. We should think of it as a reading-readiness line. Its books would have the same trim size but be thirty-six pages instead of seventy-two. And he wanted a whole new feel—a whole new look.

"We're very excited about it," he continued. "There's nothing like it on the market. We think it can be even bigger than Beginner Books. I definitely want you guys in on it. So put the scout thing aside and see what you can come up with for the new line. Remember, it's called Bright and Early Books, so think very, very young.

"And, oh yes," he added in an aside that sent our hearts down into our shoes. "Don't do bears on this project. We've got enough bears for a while. Anyway, you can't do bears forever. And, look, I'm coming east in a couple weeks. Call Elma [she was the Beginner Books secretary] and set up a meeting. I'm really eager to see what you come up with."

Ted's excitement was electrifying, but the effect was short-circuited by his "don't do bears" edict. It was déjà vu all over again. And there was the news about Phyllis. "Oh, baby, what does it mean?" said Stan, which was a family catchphrase we used when we were nonplussed. It was from one of the first McDonald's commercials. We were aware of McDonald's very early on because they wanted us to do a commercial for them. The idea was to show us sketching kids at a McDonald's restaurant to demonstrate its family friendliness. However, negotiations came a cropper, and they used Susan Perl, the artist who did the ads for the kids' clothing line called Health-tex, instead. But we would have another McDonald's moment later in our career.

When Jan heard about Phyllis, she made her Eisenhower face (the face Eisenhower made when President Truman fired MacArthur). There were other changes at Random House. The Beginner Books offices were no longer in the old butler's quarters. They were in a Third Avenue skyscraper. And Jerry Harrison, a marketing expert, had taken over as president of Random House's Children's Books Division.

We had, in our innocence, thought we *could* do bears forever. But maybe Ted was right. Maybe we couldn't.

**DÉJÀ VU ALL OVER AGAIN**

Most of our story ideas are consciously thought up. But sometimes ideas come unbidden. The phrase "inside, outside, upside down" was such an idea. But what was it? What did it mean? It would make an interesting title. But where would the title take us? Ted wanted something completely different, huh? A whole new feel? A whole new look? We'd give him a look that would knock his socks off.

We noodled around until we found out what *Inside, Outside, Upside Down* was about. It was about a red gorilla who sat *inside* a hollow tree, a crow wearing a magenta beret who was *outside* sitting on a branch, and a two-toed sloth who was hanging *upside down* from a limb. Ted wanted different. We'd give him different. We took the red gorilla, the crow with the magenta beret, and the two-toed sloth and sent them on a topsy-turvy trip to town. When they arrived, they proclaimed, "We went to town! Inside, outside, upside down!"

We fetched it up to New York and set it before Ted. "Wow!" he said as he leafed through it. "Fabulous! A red gorilla and a bird with a beret and an upside-down guy—I love 'em! But I've been talking to the salesmen and they think that since your bears are so well established, we ought to have at least one bear book in the new line. But this is a great concept. Maybe you can convert it to bears. What do you think?" What did we think? You know that song "I Think I'm Goin' out of My Head"? That's what we thought.

The Berenstains responded to Ted's edict that they do something completely different from bears with *Inside, Outside, Upside Down*, a work featuring a red gorilla (inside), a beret-wearing crow (outside), and a two-toed sloth (upside down).

Back onto the train, back through the tunnel under the Hudson River, up out of the tunnel into the wilds of North Jersey, and back to North Philly Station. We arrived home in a deep funk. We remained so for most of the next day. Jan came out of it first. She wanted to be alone. She took a pencil and drawing pad into the yard and sat at our weathered old picnic table. By late afternoon she had penciled a whole new bear version of *Inside, Outside, Upside Down*. In fifteen pictures and sixty-six words, she told how Small Bear goes into a box (it says "This side up" on the side and has eyeholes so Small Bear can see out) that gets dollied onto a truck and taken to town. The box falls off the truck, whereupon Small Bear climbs out and runs home shouting, "Mama! Mama! I went to town inside, outside, upside down!"

*Inside, Outside, Upside Down* was published in 1968.

It has sold more than 3 million copies.

# A LINE OF OUR OWN

WE FOLLOWED *INSIDE, OUTSIDE* WITH *BEARS ON WHEELS*, a highly unconventional counting book that begins with "One bear on one wheel" (a unicycle) and works its way through permutations and combinations of bears on wheels until all participants are unseated in a cataclysmic crash, leaving "Twenty-one on none." Next came *The Berenstains' B Book*, a Mad Max of a book consisting of a single sentence in which all the words (except for some "ands," a

Big brown bear, blue bull,
beautiful baboon
    blowing bubbles
        biking backward...

"that's," and a "what") begin with the letter *B*. Just to indicate what a high old time we and Ted had perpetrating these books, here's the entire text: "Big brown bear, blue bull, beautiful baboon blowing bubbles biking backward, bump black bug's banana boxes *and* Billy Bunny's breadbasket *and* Brother Bob's baseball bus *and* Buster Beagle's banjo-bagpipe-bugle band . . . *and that's what* broke Baby Bird's balloon." We shall spare you the text of *C Is for Clown: A Circus of "C" Words,* which followed *The Berenstains' B Book,* but you have our assurance that it is just as nutty. Between *B* and *C* we published *Bears in the Night,* a spooky book for tiny tots. All of them were multimillion best-sellers.

We have worked with many fine editors. Janet Schulman, who was editor of our non-Seuss books for many years, is a wonderful editor and has been a warm friend to us and our bears. Nor is our present editor, publisher Kate Klimo, exactly a tomato can. Not only is she a superb editor and a fine writer in her own right, she is wise in the ways of the ever-changing children's market. And in addition to having great publishing savvy, associate publisher Cathy Goldsmith is merely the best art director we've ever worked with.

Stan and Jan with Ted and Maurice Sendak at Dr. Seuss's eightieth birthday party at the Jockey Club in New York City.

But notwithstanding the above encomia, Theodor Seuss Geisel was unique. He wasn't trying to expand the envelope. As far as Ted was concerned, there *was* no envelope. We doubt that the Bears would have happened except for Ted, nor is it likely that any of the books we did with him would have been published except under his remarkable editorship.

**DOWN A SUNNY DIRT ROAD**

Although paperbacks had been a major and rapidly growing factor in the publishing business since the late forties, they did not become an important factor in the children's picture book market until Ole Risom came from Golden Books to Random House and created the Pictureback line (a play on "paperback"). *The Berenstain Bears' New Baby,* an early Pictureback title, was an auspicious event for us for a number of reasons. It was the first Bears paperback, it brought Sister Bear into the family (changing Small Bear's name to Brother Bear after that), and it gave us the opportunity to

do stories about ordinary, everyday family experiences. An event depicted in *New Baby* came directly from something that happened when Jan was pregnant with Michael. Jan often took Leo onto her lap for book readings. Over time Leo noticed that Jan's lap was getting smaller. This provided an excellent opportunity to tell him why. Leo, a model of generosity and equanimity, found the news both interesting and acceptable. Shortly after Michael was born, Leo climbed onto Jan's lap and was delighted to find that it had returned. "Mommy," he said, "you got your lap back!"

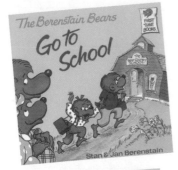

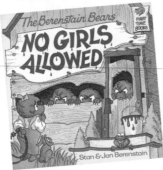

*The Berenstain Bears Go to School,* our second title for Ole, was also a family experience book. It dealt in a gentle and reassuring way with the potentially worrisome experience of starting school. We were very comfortable doing these family experience books and understood that they were doing well. What we didn't know was that *New Baby* and *Go to School* had shot to number one on the best-seller lists when they were published. We found that out inadvertently during a promotional trip to the Minneapolis area, which was the home base of B. Dalton Booksellers, a major national chain. "Well, how do you like having number one best-sellers two books in a row?" we were asked.

*Hmm,* we thought on the airplane trip home. *Why don't we do a whole series of family experience books?*

We arranged to go up to New York to pitch the idea to Jerry Harrison, who was running the division at the time. He was a large, bearlike man, who, we understood from Janet Schulman, was predisposed toward our bears. We had lunch at Christ Cella, a famously expensive restaurant, which, oddly, had sawdust on its floor. But sawdust notwithstanding, we enthusiastically launched into our pitch for "First Time Books" (Jan thought up the name and logo). It would, we said, be a first-experience series that would deal with the various and sundry crises and contretemps families have to deal with: going to the doctor, visiting the dentist, sibling squabbling, separation anxiety, the trauma of moving, the trouble with money. After all, *New Baby* and *Go to School* had each shot to number one on the best-seller list on publication as Picturebacks. So there was clearly a market for such a series. There wasn't anything like it on the market, etc., etc.

We were still selling like steam engines when we became aware that Jerry was holding up his hand like a traffic cop. We stopped pitching.

"Fellows and girls," said Jerry, "I said I thought it was a good idea five minutes ago. I said I'd put a contract together and send it over to Sterling."

We were so surprised and pleased that we forgot to ask about the sawdust.

First Time Books proved successful from the start. When we began the line, we thought there might be as many as ten first-time experiences that could work as books. But we found that ordinary, everyday experiences were a much richer lode than we had anticipated. There are now fifty-three First Time Books in print, with many more scheduled. The line includes such titles as *Moving Day, In the Dark, The Messy Room, The Truth, Mama's New Job, The Trouble with Friends, Too Much Junk Food, The Bad Dream, Too Much Teasing, The Bad Habit, The Homework Hassle, The Blame Game,* and many others, all conveniently listed on the inside front cover of each and every First Time Book.

First Time Books were so successful that they generated an extraordinary range of ancillary activities, including a series of prime-time Berenstain Bears specials on NBC, two years of Saturday morning Berenstain Bears shows on CBS (most of which have worked their way into the home video market), and worldwide TV distribution.

There followed a succession of Berenstain Bears Happy Meals from McDonald's (in the course of one

four-week Happy Meals promotion, McDonald's sold 35 million Berenstain Bears figurines—and they had to send a 747 to China for 4 million more Sister Bears because they ran out), themed Berenstain Bears areas in amusement parks in five states, toys, dolls, games, puzzles, stickers, cookies, candy, and commercial tie-ins with the likes of Texaco ("A Berenstain Bears book for a buck with a fill-up!") and Kellogg's ("A Berenstain Bears book free with four proofs-of-purchase"). And, admittedly, it's breathtaking to know that our funny, furry bears are seen on television in fifty countries (we wonder what they think of them in China, Sri Lanka, Kuwait, Gabon, and Bophuthatswana). It's all quite astonishing to a cartooning couple who long ago set out to do a couple of funny kids' books. But the mad multitudinousness of it all, while appreciated, is not what we're about. What we're about is number two pencils, yellow legal pads, nib pens, watercolors, Winsor Newton brushes, series 500 two-ply Bristol board, and a family of bears who live down a sunny dirt road deep in Bear Country.

Michael, left, at his drawing board. Leo, right, at his word processor.

# FAMILY BUSINESS

A CRISIS OCCURS AT THE END OF THE FIRST ACT of "The Berenstain Bears' Easter Surprise," a TV special we did for NBC. Boss Bunny, overwhelmed with the burgeoning responsibilities of Easter, goes on strike, stating his case as follows:

> *"I'm old and tired,*
> *Bent and stooped.*
> *I'm p-double o p e-d,*
> *POOPED!"*

(For the proper effect, the last word should be piped in falsetto.)

We weren't quite as overwhelmed as Boss Bunny, but we were beginning to bend a bit under the demand for more and more books about the Berenstain Bears. There were more ideas and opportunities to explore than we could handle. A new strain had come into the steady stream of fan mail. "Why," young fans were repeatedly asking, "don't you do some chapter books for us older kids who are too big for your picture books?" What, we wondered, were "chapter books"? Our editor informed us that they simply were books with chapters (as distinct from picture books, which were chapterless).

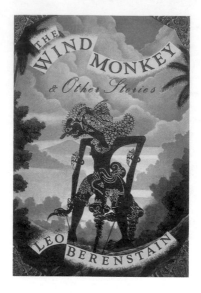

Son Michael, a successful author/illustrator of children's books in his own right, had already joined Team Berenstain as illustrator/art director.

We three prevailed upon son Leo, who had just published a well-received book of short stories about his experiences as a research scientist in the Borneo jungle, to come down an age peg and help create Big Chapter Books (again, with the logo designed by Jan).

So with Leo as writer and Michael as illustrator/cover artist (and with a little help from Mom and Dad), the brothers Berenstain developed a full line of illustrated mini-novels for older children who might have outgrown our picture books but had not outgrown our Bears.

Big Chapter Books deal with a broad range of prepubescent experience: the overweening sports dad in *Phenom in the Family*, juvenile drug use in *Drug Free Zone*, boy-girl relationships in *New Girl in Town*, crime and punishment in *Red-Handed Thief*, environmental concerns in *Showdown at Chainsaw Gap*, and other similarly "advanced" subjects, even including the primally controversial subject of guns in *No Guns Allowed*. The premise is that cubs (and kids) should not be permitted to bring guns to school. The book was widely and favorably received. But even that modest premise elicited some startling e-mail from gun enthusiasts who hadn't seen, much less read, the book.

More recently, we and the brothers Berenstain have developed an additional chapter book line that is designed to split the age difference between First Time Books and Big Chapter Books. It will be part of Random House's Stepping Stone line and will employ the entire easy-to-read armamentarium: simple language, short declarative sentences, and the open look of short paragraphs.

The business press abounds with cautionary tales about the hazards inherent in conducting a family business: litigation, estrangement, blood feuds. We don't wish to tempt fate, but as far as the family Berenstain is concerned, so far, so good.

As for the future, one of our grandchildren can already draw pretty good bears.

E. Berenstain

# PLAYING FAVORITES

WE ARE FREQUENTLY ASKED if we have a favorite among our many books. Our answer is that we do not. We do, however, have favorite scenes, subjects, and nuances. Here is a folio of some of them along with comments on why.

Below: In introducing grandparents into the series in *The Berenstain Bears and the Week at Grandma's,* we took pains to make them paragons of munificence and virtue. Did the fact that we are grandparents have anything to do with that? You're darned right!

No matter how you hope,
No matter how you try,
You can't make truth
Out of a lie.

Above: From the beginning of the series, each First Time Book has been introduced by a rhymed epigraph. This one sets the tone for *The Berenstain Bears and the Truth.*

Left: Too-Tall Grizzly, schoolyard bully and general all-around bad influence, was introduced in *Double Dare.* Here, he is trying to tempt Brother Bear into the ways of watermelon stealing. The watermelons are striped because we couldn't make the solid green ones work. They insisted on looking like misshapen bowling balls.

Above: Sibling rivalry is one of our specialties. The fact that Brother and Sister sleep in a bunk bed gives their relationship resonance in *Get in a Fight*.

Above: Camp director Grizzly Bob conducts a powwow by firelight in full Native American regalia in *Go to Camp* (particular attention is called to Stan's fire, which isn't half bad).

Papa banged on the table and shouted as only he could shout. But nothing really seemed to do any good.

Above: Mrs. Grizzle made her first appearance in *The Sitter*. She is largely based on the film actress Marjorie Main, progenitor of the classic "harridan with a heart of gold" role.

Above: We got a certain amount of parental satisfaction by having Papa Bear bang down so hard on the table that plates, silverware, and a honey pot jump in *Forget Their Manners*.

And she got into the strangest positions.

Also, of course, she grew. She grew so much that the Bear family started calling her Lady instead of Little Lady. And, like all puppies, she loved to chew.

Above: Providing Jan with an opportunity to draw cute puppies wasn't the only reason we did *The Trouble with Pets,* but it *was* one of them.

Above: *Moving Day* was one of the first First Time Books, but the reason this painting made our "favorite" folio is that it included the best stone bridge we've ever done.

Above: The Bears' tree house never looked better than it did in *The Berenstain Bears Meet Santa Bear.*

As they drove along, they passed the lighted windows of the Beartown Department Store. They were beautifully decorated for Christmas. There was window after window of new toys and games, new things for the house, and the very latest thing in fishing poles.

But the members of the Bear family were so filled with special thoughts about helping others that they hardly noticed the wonderful things in the windows...

Then, after a fond farewell look at their old home, the Bear family said good-bye to their friends and neighbors, got into their car, and headed down the mountain. The big moving truck followed

Below: The wonder of attics figured in both our young lives. Here, Papa Bear has brought Sister up into the tree house attic to find his old night-light to help her overcome her fear of the dark in *The Berenstain Bears in the Dark*.

Below: Christmas Eve in Bear Country looks a lot like Christmas Eve in downtown Philadelphia in the 1930s (*The Berenstain Bears Think of Those in Need*).

Above: A new cub joins the Bear family in *The Berenstain Bears and Baby Makes Five*. Sister overcomes her jealousy and acknowledges that the new arrival is really "kind of cute."

# SUMMING UP

WE ARE OFTEN ASKED, "What is it like doing the Berenstain Bears?"

Though we don't lay claim to our bears having any great importance in any larger scheme of things, they are certainly important to us. Next to our sons and their families, and each other, they are the most important thing in our lives. They wake up with us every morning. They send us to bed every night. And almost every day we work with them as they try to cope with the problems and questions attendant to everyday life: small problems like those explored in books such as *Get the Gimmies* and *Too Much Teasing,* and big questions like the one posed in *The Big Question.* (The big question is "Mama, what's God?")

So what is it like doing the Berenstain Bears?

It's gratifying. We would be lying if we didn't acknowledge that it's deeply satisfying to have created something that, at the very least, has entertained millions, and has on occasion been helpful to those same millions in some small way.

It's exciting. It's somewhat awkward to admit it, but though we have done an embarrassingly large number of books about our bears (more than two hundred at last count), opening a FedEx or UPS package and going through a new Bears book for the very first time is just as exciting today as it was two hundred books ago.

It's constantly surprising. A teacher at the Friends school that our grandchildren attend returns from an outreach trip to the high Andes, where she snapped a picture of a Peruvian father reading a Spanish-language version of one of our books to his child. We receive a letter from a class of schoolchildren in New Zealand. It begins, "Dear Mr. and Mrs. Berenstain. We are a third-grade class in New Zealand. All our fathers are shepherds. . . ."

We receive an e-mail from the grandmother of a five-year-old who has been diagnosed as amblyopic and is upset and embarrassed because she has to wear an eye patch. Boy, did she come to the right place! Stan e-mails the granddaughter, saying that he suffers from the same condition and advising her that, though he understands her feelings, she should do her best to wear the patch. We receive an e-mail from the grandmother informing us that the little girl has hung our e-mail on her wall and is wearing the eye patch with reasonably good grace.

It's humbling—so much so that it's difficult to talk about, or even write about, without choking up. A package arrives containing a few of our books and a letter from a school librarian that tells about a little boy who is ill. He is so weak that he can't participate in classwork. But he wants to be in school, so he comes to the library every day and looks at his favorite Berenstain Bears books. Would we please autograph the books? We autograph them and add a few more for good measure.

*The New York Times Magazine* does a story on the aftermath of the tragic and hideous bombing of the Murrah Federal Building, in Oklahoma City, in which 168 people—many of them children— were killed. A photo shows a section of the cyclone fence that was installed around the building. Hanging on the fence are tributes memorializing the dead children. Prominent among them is a small stuffed Sister Bear doll.

We get a call from Kate's assistant. She has just received a call from the Sloan-Kettering cancer hospital in New York City. A little girl is stricken with cancer. Her dying wish is for a Sister Bear doll. We hastily stumble down into our stygian cellar, dig through boxes, and find a Sister Bear doll. We FedEx it to Ms. Somebody in the Department of Patient Services at Sloan-Kettering. We are informed later that the little girl died with Sister Bear in her arms.

Another question we are often asked arises from the

perception that at this point in our lives, we could easily retire. The comment usually runs along the following lines: "I know what I would do if I were in your position. I'd retire and travel." The answer to that question is twofold. Why in the world would we retire? We thrive on what we do and we're going to keep on doing it, we say (only partially tongue in cheek), until we get it wrong. As for travel—we *do* travel. Extensively. We go to a lovely, salubrious place where honeybees hum, where rainbow trout match rainbow skies, where the rivers run clean and the air is sweet, where there's beauty around every bend in the sunny dirt road. It's a wonderful place. It's called Bear Country.

We go there every day.

# BIBLIOGRAPHY

(All titles published by Random House
unless otherwise noted.)

## ADVICE

*The Berenstains' Baby Book*, Macmillan, 1951.
*The Facts of Life for Grownups*, Dell, 1963, also
    published as *What Doctor Freud Didn't Tell
    You.*
*How to Teach Your Children About Sex . . . Without
    Making a Complete Fool of Yourself*, McCall,
    1970.
*How to Teach Your Children About God . . .
    Without Actually Scaring Them Out of Their
    Wits*, McCall, 1971.
*What Your Parents Never Told You About Being a
    Mom or Dad*, Crown, 1995.

## BOARD BOOKS

**Berenstain Baby Bears**
*Berenstain Baby Bears: My New Bed*, 1999.
*Berenstain Baby Bears: My Potty and I*, 1999.
*Berenstain Baby Bears: My Trusty Car Seat*, 1999.
*Berenstain Baby Bears: Pacifier Days*, 1999.
*Berenstain Baby Bears: Me First! Me First!*, 2000.
*Berenstain Baby Bears: My Every Day Book*, 2000.

**Peek-a-Board Books**
*The Berenstain Bears in Big Bear City*, 1996.
*The Berenstain Bears: Yike! Yike! Where's My Trike?*,
    1996.
*Home Sweet Tree*, 1997.

## BOOKS WITH AUDIOCASSETTE

**Beginner Book and Cassette Library**
*The Bears' Vacation*, 1987.
*The Bear Detectives: The Case of the Missing
    Pumpkin*, 1988.
*The Bears' Christmas*, 1988.

**First Time Book and Cassette Library**
*The Berenstain Bears and the Sitter*, 1985.
*The Berenstain Bears Go to School*, 1985.
*The Berenstain Bears Go to the Doctor*, 1985.
*The Berenstain Bears' New Baby*, 1985.
*The Berenstain Bears Visit the Dentist*, 1985.
*The Berenstain Bears Forget Their Manners*, 1986.
*The Berenstain Bears Learn About Strangers*, 1986.
*The Berenstain Bears Get in a Fight*, 1987.
*The Berenstain Bears and Too Much TV*, 1989.
*The Berenstain Bears Go to Camp*, 1989.
*The Berenstain Bears Meet Santa Bear*, 1989.
*The Berenstain Bears and Too Much Vacation*, 1990.
*The Berenstain Bears Go Out for the Team*, 1991.

## CHAPTER BOOKS

**The Berenstain Bear Scout Chapter Books**
(published by Little Apple, Scholastic; illustrated by
Michael Berenstain)
*The Berenstain Bear Scouts and the Coughing
    Catfish*, 1995.
*The Berenstain Bear Scouts and the Humongous
    Pumpkin*, 1995.

*The Berenstain Bear Scouts in Giant Bat Cave*,
    1995.
*The Berenstain Bear Scouts Meet Bigpaw*, 1995.
*The Berenstain Bear Scouts and the Sci-Fi Pizza*,
    1996.
*The Berenstain Bear Scouts and the Terrible Talking
    Termite*, 1996.
*The Berenstain Bear Scouts: Ghost Versus Ghost*,
    1996.
*The Berenstain Bear Scouts Save That Backscratcher*,
    1996.
*The Berenstain Bear Scouts and the Ice Monster*,
    1997.
*The Berenstain Bear Scouts and the Magic Crystal
    Caper*, 1997.
*The Berenstain Bear Scouts and the Run-Amuck
    Robot*, 1997.
*The Berenstain Bear Scouts and the Sinister Smoke
    Ring*, 1997.
*The Berenstain Bear Scouts and the Evil Eye*, 1998.
*The Berenstain Bear Scouts and the Really Big
    Disaster*, 1998.
*The Berenstain Bear Scouts and the Ripoff Queen*,
    1998.
*The Berenstain Bear Scouts Scream Their Heads Off*,
    1998.

**Big Chapter Books**
(with Leo and Michael Berenstain)
*The Berenstain Bears Accept No Substitutes*, 1993.
*The Berenstain Bears and the Drug Free Zone*, 1993.
*The Berenstain Bears and the Female Fullback*, 1993.
*The Berenstain Bears and the Nerdy Nephew*, 1993.
*The Berenstain Bears and the New Girl in Town*,
    1993.
*The Berenstain Bears and the Red-Handed Thief*,
    1993.
*The Berenstain Bears and the Wheelchair
    Commando*, 1993.
*The Berenstain Bears Gotta Dance!*, 1993.
*The Berenstain Bears and the Dress Code*, 1994.
*The Berenstain Bears and the Galloping Ghost*,
    1994.
*The Berenstain Bears and the Giddy Grandma*,
    1994.
*The Berenstain Bears and the School Scandal Sheet*,
    1994.
*The Berenstain Bears at Camp Crush*, 1994.
*The Berenstain Bears and the Showdown at
    Chainsaw Gap*, 1995.
*The Berenstain Bears in the Freaky Funhouse*, 1995.
*The Berenstain Bears' Media Madness*, 1995.
*The Berenstain Bears at the Teen Rock Cafe*, 1996.
*The Berenstain Bears in Maniac Mansion*, 1996.
*The Berenstain Bears and Queenie's Crazy Crush*,
    1997.
*The Berenstain Bears and the Bermuda Triangle*,
    1997.
*The Berenstain Bears and the Ghost of the Auto
    Graveyard*, 1997.
*The Berenstain Bears and the Haunted Hayride*,
    1997.

*The Berenstain Bears and the Big Date*, 1998.
*The Berenstain Bears and the Love Match*, 1998.
*The Berenstain Bears and the Perfect Crime (Almost)*, 1998.
*The Berenstain Bears Go Platinum*, 1998.
*The Berenstain Bears and the G-Rex Bones*, 1999.
*The Berenstain Bears Go Hollywood*, 1999.
*The Berenstain Bears in the Wax Museum*, 1999.
*The Berenstain Bears: Lost in Cyberspace*, 1999.
*The Berenstain Bears and No Guns Allowed*, 2000.
*The Berenstain Bears and the Great Ant Attack*, 2000.
*The Berenstain Bears: Phenom in the Family*, 2000.

**Merit Badge Mysteries**
(published by Cartwheel Books, Scholastic; illustrated by Michael Berenstain)
*The Berenstain Bear Scouts and the Missing Merit Badges*, 1998.
*The Berenstain Bear Scouts and the Search for Naughty Ned*, 1998.
*The Berenstain Bear Scouts and the Stinky Milk Mystery*, 1999.
*The Berenstain Bear Scouts and the White Water Mystery*, 1999.

**Stepping Stone Books**
(with Leo and Michael Berenstain)
*The Goofy, Goony Guy*, 2001.
*The Haunted Lighthouse*, 2001.
*The Runamuck Dog Show*, 2001.
*The Wrong Crowd*, 2001.
*Ride Like the Wind*, 2002.

## HUMOR
*Sister* (cartoons), Schuman, 1952.
*Tax-Wise*, Schuman, 1952.
*Marital Blitz*, Dutton, 1954.
*Baby Makes Four*, Macmillan, 1957.
*It's All in the Family*, Dutton, 1958.
*Lover Boy*, Macmillan, 1958.
*And Beat Him When He Sneezes*, McGraw Hill, 1960, reprinted as *Have a Baby, My Wife Just Had a Cigar*.
*Bedside Lover Boy*, Dell, 1960.
*Call Me Mrs.*, Macmillian, 1961, also published as *I Love You Kid, But Oh My Wife*.
*It's Still in the Family*, Dutton, 1961.
*Office Lover Boy*, Dell, 1962.
*Flipsville-Squaresville*, Delacorte, 1965.
*Mr. Dirty vs. Mrs. Clean*, Dell, 1967.
*You Could Diet Laughing*, Dell, 1969.
*Be Good or I'll Belt Ya!*, Dell, 1970.
*Education Impossible*, Dell, 1970.
*Never Trust Anyone over 13*, Bantam, 1970.
*Are Parents for Real?*, Bantam, 1972.
*It's All in the Family 2*, 1985.

## NONFICTION
*The Bears' Nature Guide*, 1975, reissued as *The Berenstain Bears' Nature Guide*, 1984.
*The Berenstain Bears' Science Fair*, 1977.
*The Bears' Activity Book*, 1979.

*The Berenstain Bears' Make and Do Book*, 1984.
*The Berenstain Bears' Science & Nature Super Treasury*, 1985, reissued as *The Berenstain Bears' Big Book of Science and Nature*, 1997.

## NOVELTY
*Papa's Pizza: A Berenstain Bear Sniffy Book*, 1978.
*The Berenstain Bears' Storybook Tree House*, 1982.
*The Berenstain Bears' Toy Time*, 1985.
*The Berenstain Bears' Bath Book*, 1986.
*The Berenstain Bears' New Clothes*, 1997.

## PICTURE BOOKS
*The Berenstain Bears' Counting Book*, 1976.
*The Berenstain Bears' Christmas Tree*, 1980.
*The Berenstain Bears: Coughing Catfish*, 1988.
*The Berenstain Bears' Thanksgiving*, Cartwheel Books, Scholastic, 1997.
*The Berenstain Bears' Comic Valentine*, Cartwheel Books, Scholastic, 1998.
*The Berenstain Bears' Easter Surprise*, Cartwheel Books, Scholastic, 1998.
*The Berenstain Bears Play Ball*, Cartwheel Books, Scholastic, 1998.

**First First Time Books**
*The Berenstain Bears Are a Family*, 1991.
*The Berenstain Bears at the Super-Duper Market*, 1991.
*The Berenstain Bears' Four Seasons*, 1991.
*The Berenstain Bears Say Good Night*, 1991.

**First Time Books®**
*The Berenstain Bears' Nursery Tales*, 1973.
*The Berenstain Bears' New Baby*, 1974.
*The Berenstain Bears Go to School*, 1978.
*The Berenstain Bears and the Sitter*, 1981.
*The Berenstain Bears Go to the Doctor*, 1981.
*The Berenstain Bears' Moving Day*, 1981.
*The Berenstain Bears Visit the Dentist*, 1981.
*The Berenstain Bears Get in a Fight*, 1982.
*The Berenstain Bears Go to Camp*, 1982.
*The Berenstain Bears in the Dark*, 1982.
*The Berenstain Bears and the Messy Room*, 1983.
*The Berenstain Bears and the Truth*, 1983.
*The Berenstain Bears' Trouble with Money*, 1983.
*The Berenstain Bears and Mama's New Job*, 1984.
*The Berenstain Bears and Too Much TV*, 1984.
*The Berenstain Bears Meet Santa Bear*, 1984.
*The Berenstain Bears and Too Much Junk Food*, 1985.
*The Berenstain Bears Forget Their Manners*, 1985.
*The Berenstain Bears Learn About Strangers*, 1985.
*The Berenstain Bears and the Week at Grandma's*, 1986.
*The Berenstain Bears and Too Much Birthday*, 1986.
*The Berenstain Bears Get Stage Fright*, 1986.
*The Berenstain Bears: No Girls Allowed*, 1986.
*The Berenstain Bears and the Bad Habit*, 1987.
*The Berenstain Bears and the Trouble with Friends*, 1987.
*The Berenstain Bears Go Out for the Team*, 1987.
*The Berenstain Bears' Trouble at School*, 1987.

*The Berenstain Bears and the Bad Dream*, 1988.
*The Berenstain Bears and the Double Dare*, 1988.
*The Berenstain Bears Get the Gimmies*, 1988.
*The Berenstain Bears and the In-Crowd*, 1989.
*The Berenstain Bears and Too Much Vacation*, 1989.
*The Berenstain Bears Trick or Treat*, 1989.
*The Berenstain Bears and the Prize Pumpkin*, 1990.
*The Berenstain Bears and the Slumber Party*, 1990.
*The Berenstain Bears' Trouble with Pets*, 1990.
*The Berenstain Bears Don't Pollute (Anymore)*, 1991.
*The Berenstain Bears and the Trouble with
    Grownups*, 1992.
*The Berenstain Bears and Too Much Pressure*, 1993.
*The Berenstain Bears and the Bully*, 1994.
*The Berenstain Bears' New Neighbors*, 1994.
*The Berenstain Bears and the Green-Eyed Monster*,
    1995.
*The Berenstain Bears and Too Much Teasing*, 1995.
*The Berenstain Bears Count Their Blessings*, 1995.
*The Berenstain Bears and the Blame Game*, 1997.
*The Berenstain Bears and the Homework Hassle*,
    1997.
*The Berenstain Bears Get Their Kicks*, 1998.
*The Berenstain Bears Lend a Helping Hand*, 1998.
*The Berenstain Bears and the Big Question*, 1999.
*The Berenstain Bears' Mad, Mad, Mad Toy Craze*,
    1999.
*The Berenstain Bears Think of Those in Need*, 1999.
*The Berenstain Bears and Baby Makes Five*, 2000.
*The Berenstain Bears and the Big Blooper*, 2000.
*The Birds, the Bees, and the Berenstain Bears*, 2000.
*The Berenstain Bears and the Excuse Note*, 2001.
*The Berenstain Bears' Dollars and Sense*, 2001.
*The Berenstain Bears and the Real Easter Eggs*,
    2002.
*The Berenstain Bears' Report Card Trouble*, 2002.

**First Time Do-It! Books**
*Cook It!*, 1996.
*Draw It!*, 1996.
*Fly It!*, 1996.
*Grow It!*, 1996.

**First Time Workbooks**
*The Berenstain Bears and the Messy Room*, 1998.
*The Berenstain Bears Get the Gimmies*, 1998.
*The Berenstain Bears in the Dark*, 1998.
*The Berenstain Bears' Trouble with Money*, 1998.

**Jellybean Books**
*The Berenstain Bears Get the Don't Haftas*, 1998.
*The Berenstain Bears Get the Screamies*, 1998.
*The Berenstain Bears Get the Noisies*, 1999.
*The Berenstain Bears Get the Scaredies*, 1999.
*The Berenstain Bears Get the Twitchies*, 2000.

**Mini-Storybooks**
*The Berenstain Bears and the Wild, Wild Honey*,
    1983.
*The Berenstain Bears Go Fly a Kite*, 1983.
*The Berenstain Bears' Soccer Star*, 1983.
*The Berenstain Bears to the Rescue*, 1983.
*The Berenstain Bears and the Big Election*, 1984.
*The Berenstain Bears and the Dinosaurs*, 1984.

*The Berenstain Bears and the Neighborly Skunk*,
    1984.
*The Berenstain Bears Shoot the Rapids*, 1984.

**READERS**
**Beginner Books**
*The Big Honey Hunt*, 1962.
*The Bike Lesson*, 1964.
*The Bears' Picnic*, 1966.
*The Bear Scouts*, 1967.
*The Bears' Vacation*, 1968.
*The Bears' Christmas*, 1970.
*The Bears' Almanac*, 1973.
*The Bear Detectives*, 1975.
*The Berenstain Bears and the Missing Dinosaur
    Bone*, 1980.
*The Berenstain Bears: That Stump Must Go*, 2000.

**Bright and Early Books**
*Inside, Outside, Upside Down*, 1968.
*Bears on Wheels*, 1969.
*Old Hat, New Hat*, 1970.
*The B Book*, 1971.
*Bears in the Night*, 1971.
*C Is for Clown*, 1972, reissued as *The C Book*, 1997.
*He Bear, She Bear*, 1974.
*The Berenstain Bears and the Spooky Old Tree*,
    1978.
*The Berenstain Bears on the Moon*, 1985.
*The A Book*, 1997.

**First Time Readers**
*The Berenstain Bears and the Big Road Race*, 1987.
*The Berenstain Bears and the Missing Honey*, 1987.
*The Berenstain Bears Blaze a Trail*, 1987.
*The Berenstain Bears on the Job*, 1987.
*The Berenstain Kids: I Love Colors*, 1987.
*The Day of the Dinosaur*, illustrated by Michael
    Berenstain, 1987.
*After the Dinosaurs*, illustrated by Michael
    Berenstain, 1988.
*The Berenstain Bears and the Ghost of the Forest*,
    1988.
*The Berenstain Bears: Ready, Get Set, Go!*, 1988.

**Step into Reading Books**
*The Berenstain Bears: Big Bear, Small Bear*, 1998.
*The Berenstain Bears by the Sea*, 1998.
*The Berenstain Bears Ride the Thunderbolt*, 1998.
*The Berenstain Bears Catch the Bus*, 1999.
*The Berenstain Bears Go Up and Down*, 1999.
*The Berenstain Bears in the House of Mirrors*, 1999.
*The Berenstain Bears and the Escape of the Bogg
    Brothers, A Bear Detectives Mystery*, 2000.
*The Berenstain Bears Go In and Out*, 2000.
*The Berenstain Bears and the Missing Watermelon
    Money, A Bear Detectives Mystery*, 2001.
*The Berenstain Bears and the Tic-Tac-Toe Mystery,
    A Bear Detectives Mystery*, 2001.

**VIDEOCASSETTES**
*The Berenstain Bears Meet Bigpaw*, Embassy Home
    Video, 1980.

**DOWN A SUNNY DIRT ROAD**

*The Berenstain Bears Volume 1: The Messy Room, The Terrible Talking Termite, Life with Papa Teacher,* Columbia TriStar Home Entertainment, 1986.

*The Berenstain Bears Volume 2: The Truth, Save the Bees, The Forbidden Cave,* Columbia TriStar Home Entertainment, 1986.

*The Berenstain Bears Volume 3: Learn About Strangers, The Disappearing Honey, The Substitute Teacher,* Columbia TriStar Home Entertainment, 1986.

*The Berenstain Bears Volume 4: Forget Their Manners, The Bigpaw Problem, The Cat's Meow,* Columbia TriStar Home Entertainment, 1986.

*The Berenstain Bears Volume 5: In the Dark, The Wicked Weasel Spell, The Mystery Mansion,* Columbia TriStar Home Entertainment, 1986.

*The Berenstain Bears Volume 6: Too Much Birthday, Bonkers over Honkers, Go Fly a Kite,* Columbia TriStar Home Entertainment, 1985.

*The Berenstain Bears and Cupid's Surprise,* Kids Klassics, 1989.

*The Berenstain Bears and the Messy Room,* Random House Home Video, 1989.

*The Berenstain Bears and the Trouble with Friends,* Random House Home Video, 1989.

*The Berenstain Bears and the Truth,* Random House Home Video, 1989.

*The Berenstain Bears and Too Much Birthday,* Random House Home Video, 1989.

*The Berenstain Bears' Easter Surprise,* Kids Klassics, 1989.

*The Berenstain Bears Forget Their Manners,* Random House Home Video, 1989.

*The Berenstain Bears Get in a Fight,* Random House Home Video, 1989.

*The Berenstain Bears Get Stage Fright,* Random House Home Video, 1989.

*The Berenstain Bears in the Dark,* Random House Home Video, 1989.

*The Berenstain Bears Learn About Strangers,* Random House Home Video, 1989.

*The Berenstain Bears: No Girls Allowed,* Random House Home Video, 1989.

*The Berenstain Bears and the Missing Dinosaur Bone,* Random House Home Video, 1990.

*The Berenstain Bears' Christmas,* Random House Home Video, 1990.

*The Berenstain Bears Play Ball,* Kids Klassics, 1990.

*The Berenstain Bears Volume 7: The Trouble with Friends, Ring the Bell, The Neighborly Skunk,* Columbia TriStar Home Entertainment, 2001.

*The Berenstain Bears Volume 8: The Missing Dinosaur Bone, To the Rescue, Save the Farm,* Columbia TriStar Home Entertainment, 2001.

# CHRONOLOGY

**1923**
Janice Grant born July 26 in Philadelphia,
Pennsylvania.
Stanley Berenstain born September 29 in
Philadelphia, Pennsylvania.

**1941–42**
Stan attends Philadelphia Museum School of
Industrial Art.

**1941–43 & 44–45**
Jan attends Philadelphia Museum School of Industrial
Art.

**1942–46**
Stan serves in U.S. Army as a medical artist in WWII.

**1943–44**
Jan spends a year as an aircraft riveter and draftsman
during WWII.

**1945–47**
Jan teaches drawing and painting at School of
Industrial Art. Also paints giftware.

**1946–47**
Stan attends Pennsylvania Academy for the Fine Arts.

**1946**
Stan and Jan marry—live in Philadelphia until 1949.

**1947**
Stan and Jan sell their first cartoons to *The Saturday
Evening Post* and *Collier's*.

**1948**
First son, Leo, is born.

**1948–56**
Create series of covers and interior spreads for
*Collier's*.

**1951**
*The Berenstains' Baby Book* published.
Second son, Michael, is born.

**1952**
"Sister" (*Collier's* cartoon) and *Tax-Wise* published.

**1954**
*Marital Blitz* published.

**1956**
Create *It's All in the Family*, cartoon feature for
*McCall's* that appears monthly through 1969.

**1957**
*Baby Makes Four* published.

**1958**
*It's All in the Family* (collection) published.
*Lover Boy* published.

**1960**
*And Beat Him When He Sneezes* published.
*Bedside Lover Boy* published.

School Bell Award for distinguished service in the
interpretation of education in a national
magazine (*Better Homes and Gardens:* "How
to Undermine Junior's Teacher").

**1961**
*Call Me Mrs.* published.
*It's Still in the Family* published.

**1962**
Publish their first children's book, *The Big Honey
Hunt.*
*Office Lover Boy* published.
Stan receives the Golden Anniversary Alumni Award
of Merit from West Philadelphia High School.

**1963**
*The Facts of Life for Grownups* published.

**1964**
*The Bike Lesson* published.

**1965**
*Flipsville-Squaresville* published.

**1966**
*The Bears' Picnic published.*

**1967**
*The Bear Scouts* published.
*Mr. Dirty vs. Mrs. Clean* published.
Stanley and Janice Berenstain manuscript collection is
established at Syracuse University.

**1968**
*The Bears' Vacation* published.
*Inside, Outside, Upside Down* published (British
Book Centre Honor Book).

**1969**
*Bears on Wheels* published.
*You Could Diet Laughing* published.

**1970**
*It's All in the Family* moves to *Good Housekeeping*
and appears bimonthly through 1990 with the
help of artist son Michael, who creates the
features during 1989–90.
American Institute of Graphic Arts Best Book—
*The Bear Scouts.*
*The Bears' Christmas* published.
*Be Good or I'll Belt Ya!* published.
*Education Impossible* published.
*How to Teach Your Children About Sex . . . Without
Making a Complete Fool of Yourself* published.
*Never Trust Anyone over 13* published.
*Old Hat, New Hat* published.

**1971**
*The B Book* published.
*Bears in the Night* published.
*How to Teach Your Children About God . . .
Without Actually Scaring Them Out of Their
Wits* published.

**1972**
*C Is for Clown* published.

Philadelphia Library Children's Reading Round Table (CRRT) Honor Book—*Bears in the Night.*

### 1973
*The Bears' Almanac* published.
*The Berenstain Bears' Nursery Tales* published.
Philadelphia Library CRRT Honor Book—*The Bears' Almanac.*

### 1974
*He Bear, She Bear* published.
*The Berenstain Bears' New Baby* published.
Philadelphia Library CRRT Honor Book—*He Bear, She Bear.*

### 1975
*The Bear Detectives* published.
*The Bears' Nature Guide* published.

### 1976
*The Berenstain Bears' Counting Book* published.
Philadelphia Library CRRT Honor Book—*The Bears' Nature Guide.*

### 1977
*The Berenstain Bears' Science Fair* published.
Child Study Association Book of the Year—*The Berenstain Bears' Science Fair.*

### 1978
*The Berenstain Bears and the Spooky Old Tree* published.
*The Berenstain Bears Go to School* published.
*Papa's Pizza* published.

### 1979
*The Bears' Activity Book* published.
Write and design TV special "The Berenstain Bears' Christmas Tree" for NBC.

### 1980
*The Berenstain Bears' Christmas Tree* published.
Silver Medal from International Film and TV Festival of New York, and the MIFED Silver Diploma from International Film and TV Festival of Naples, Italy, for "The Berenstain Bears' Christmas Tree."
*The Berenstain Bears and the Missing Dinosaur Bone* published (Philadelphia Library CRRT Honor Book).
Write and design TV special "The Berenstain Bears Meet Bigpaw" for NBC.

### 1981
*The Berenstain Bears and the Sitter* published.
*The Berenstain Bears Go to the Doctor* published.
*The Berenstain Bears' Moving Day* published.
*The Berenstain Bears Visit the Dentist* published.
Michigan Council of Teachers of English Young Readers Award—*Bears in the Night.*
Write and design TV special "The Berenstain Bears' Easter Surprise" for NBC.

### 1982
*The Berenstain Bears Get in a Fight* published.
*The Berenstain Bears Go to Camp* published.

*The Berenstain Bears in the Dark* published.
*The Berenstain Bears' Storybook Tree House* published.
The Drexel Citation for Children's Literature from the Drexel University School of Library and Information Science.
Philadelphia Library CRRT Honor Book—*The Berenstain Bears Visit the Dentist.*
Child Study Association Books of the Year—*The Berenstain Bears and the Sitter, The Berenstain Bears Go to the Doctor, The Berenstain Bears' Moving Day, The Berenstain Bears Visit the Dentist.*
International Reading Association (IRA) Children's Choices—*The Berenstain Bears Go to the Doctor, The Berenstain Bears Visit the Dentist.*
Ohio Library Association Teachers of English and the IRA Buckeye Award—*The Spooky Old Tree.*
Write and design TV special "The Berenstain Bears' Comic Valentine" for NBC.
International Film and TV Festival of New York Silver Medal—"The Berenstain Bears' Comic Valentine."

### 1983
*The Berenstain Bears and the Messy Room* published.
*The Berenstain Bears and the Truth* published.
*The Berenstain Bears and the Wild, Wild Honey* published.
*The Berenstain Bears Go Fly a Kite* published.
*The Berenstain Bears' Soccer Star* published.
*The Berenstain Bears to the Rescue* published.
*The Berenstain Bears' Trouble with Money* published.
IRA Children's Choices—*The Berenstain Bears Get in a Fight, The Berenstain Bears Go to Camp, The Berenstain Bears in the Dark.*
Write and design TV special "The Berenstain Bears Play Ball" for NBC.

### 1984
*The Berenstain Bears and Mama's New Job* published.
*The Berenstain Bears and the Big Election* published.
*The Berenstain Bears and the Dinosaurs* published.
*The Berenstain Bears and the Neighborly Skunk* published.
*The Berenstain Bears and Too Much TV* published.
*The Berenstain Bears Meet Santa Bear* published.
*The Berenstain Bears Shoot the Rapids* published.
IRA Children's Choices—*The Berenstain Bears and the Messy Room, The Berenstain Bears and the Truth.*

### 1985
*The Berenstain Bears and Too Much Junk Food* published.
*The Berenstain Bears Learn About Strangers* published (Philadelphia Library CRRT Honor Book).

Ohio Library Association Teachers of English and the
IRA Buckeye Award—*The Berenstain Bears and
the Messy Room*.
*The Berenstain Bears on the Moon* published.
*The Berenstain Bears' Toy Time* published.

1985–86
Write and design Berenstain Bears children's TV series
for CBS Saturday mornings.

1986
*The Berenstain Bears and the Week at Grandma's*
published.
*The Berenstain Bears and Too Much Birthday*
published.
*The Berenstain Bears Get Stage Fright* published.
*The Berenstain Bears: No Girls Allowed* published.

1987
*The Berenstain Bears and the Bad Habit* published.
*The Berenstain Bears and the Big Road Race*
published.
*The Berenstain Bears and the Missing Honey*
published.
*The Berenstain Bears and the Trouble with Friends*
published.
*The Berenstain Bears Go Out for the Team* published.
*The Berenstain Bears Blaze a Trail* published.
*The Berenstain Bears on the Job* published.
*The Berenstain Bears' Trouble at School* published.
*The Berenstain Kids: I Love Colors* published.
*The Day of the Dinosaur*, illustrated by Michael
Berenstain, published.
Arizona Young Readers Award—*The Berenstain Bears
and the Messy Room*.
IRA Children's Choice—*The Berenstain Bears: No
Girls Allowed*.
The Humanitas Certificate for Excellence in Children's
Television—"The Berenstain Bears Forget Their
Manners" (Human Family Educational and
Cultural Institute).

1988
*The Berenstain Bears and the Bad Dream* published.
*The Berenstain Bears and the Double Dare* published.
*The Berenstain Bears Get the Gimmies* published.
*After the Dinosaurs*, illustrated by Michael Berenstain,
published.
*The Berenstain Bears and the Ghost of the Forest*
published.
*The Berenstain Bears: Ready, Get Set, Go!* published.
Philadelphia Library CRRT Honor Book—*The Day of
the Dinosaur*, illustrated by Michael Berenstain.

1989
*The Berenstain Bears and the In-Crowd* published.
*The Berenstain Bears Trick or Treat* published.
Philadelphia Library CRRT Honor Book—*After the
Dinosaurs*, illustrated by Michael Berenstain.
The Ludington Award for contributions to children's
literature (Educational Paperback Association).

1990
*The Berenstain Bears and the Prize Pumpkin* published.
*The Berenstain Bears and the Slumber Party* published.

*The Berenstain Bears' Trouble with Pets* published.

1991
*The Berenstain Bears Are a Family* published.
*The Berenstain Bears at the Super-Duper Market*
published.
*The Berenstain Bears' Four Seasons* published.
*The Berenstain Bears Say Good Night* published.
*The Berenstain Bears Don't Pollute (Anymore)*
published.
Philadelphia Library CRRT Honor Book—*The
Berenstain Bears Don't Pollute (Anymore)*.

1992
*The Berenstain Bears and the Trouble with Grownups*
published.

1993
*The Berenstain Bears and Too Much Pressure*
published.
Collaborate in the creation of Big Chapter Books,
written by Leo Berenstain and illustrated by
Michael Berenstain. *The Berenstain Bears
Accept No Substitutes, The Berenstain Bears
and the Drug Free Zone, The Berenstain Bears
and the Female Fullback, The Berenstain Bears
and the Nerdy Nephew, The Berenstain Bears
and the New Girl in Town, The Berenstain
Bears and the Red-Handed Thief, The
Berenstain Bears and the Wheelchair
Commando, The Berenstain Bears Gotta Dance!*
published.
Philadelphia Library CRRT Honor Books—
*The Berenstain Bears Accept No Substitutes,
The Berenstain Bears and the Nerdy Nephew*.

1994
Big Chapter Books with Leo and Michael Berenstain
published: *The Berenstain Bears and the Dress
Code, The Berenstain Bears and the Galloping
Ghost, The Berenstain Bears and the Giddy
Grandma, The Berenstain Bears and the School
Scandal Sheet, The Berenstain Bears at Camp
Crush*.
*The Berenstain Bears and the Bully* published.
*The Berenstain Bears' New Neighbors* published.

1995
Big Chapter Books with Leo and Michael Berenstain
published: *The Berenstain Bears and the
Showdown at Chainsaw Gap, The Berenstain
Bears in the Freaky Funhouse, The Berenstain
Bears' Media Madness*.
*The Berenstain Bears and the Green-Eyed Monster*
published.
*The Berenstain Bears and Too Much Teasing*
published.
*The Berenstain Bears Count Their Blessings* published.
The Berenstain Bear Scouts books, illustrated by
Michael Berenstain, published: *The Coughing
Catfish, Giant Bat Cave, The Humongous
Pumpkin, Meet Bigpaw*.
World Wildlife Association Friends of Animals
Award—*Giant Bat Cave*.

1996
The Berenstain Bears First Time Do-It! Books
    published: *Cook It!, Draw It!, Fly It!, Grow It!*
Big Chapter Books with Leo and Michael Berenstain
    published: *The Berenstain Bears at the Teen
    Rock Cafe, The Berenstain Bears in Maniac
    Mansion.*
The Berenstain Bear Scouts books, illustrated by
    Michael Berenstain, published: *The Sci-Fi Pizza,
    The Terrible Talking Termite, Ghost Versus
    Ghost, Save That Backscratcher.*
Great Friends to Kids Award (Philadelphia Please
    Touch Museum).

1997
Big Chapter Books with Leo and Michael Berenstain
    published: *The Berenstain Bears and Queenie's
    Crazy Crush, The Berenstain Bears and the
    Bermuda Triangle, The Berenstain Bears and the
    Ghost of the Auto Graveyard, The Berenstain
    Bears and the Haunted Hayride.*
*The Berenstain Bears and the Homework Hassle*
    published.
The Berenstain Bear Scouts books, illustrated by
    Michael Berenstain, published: *The Ice Monster,
    The Magic Crystal Caper, The Run-Amuck
    Robot, The Sinister Smoke Ring* (written by Leo
    Berenstain).
The Family Channel Seal of Quality—*The Berenstain
    Bears in the Dark* CD-ROM.
*Web Award for Best Family Site*—
    www.berenstainbears.com (Web Marketing
    Association).
Award for Best Educational Resource on the Web for
    Young Children—www.berenstainbears.com
    (StudyWeb).
The State of Nevada: Senate concurrent Resolution
    Number 16 honor for achievements in children's
    literature.
Jan receives Centennial Distinguished Alumni Award
    from Radnor High School, Wayne,
    Pennsylvania.

1998
Big Chapter Books with Leo and Michael Berenstain
    published: *The Berenstain Bears and the Big
    Date, The Berenstain Bears and the Love
    Match, The Berenstain Bears and the Perfect
    Crime (Almost), The Berenstain Bears Go
    Platinum.*
*The Berenstain Bears Get Their Kicks* published.
*The Berenstain Bears Lend a Helping Hand* published.
*The Berenstain Bears: Big Bear, Small Bear* published.
*The Berenstain Bears by the Sea* published.
*The Berenstain Bears Ride the Thunderbolt* published.
The Berenstain Bear Scouts books, illustrated by
    Michael Berenstain, published: *The Evil Eye,
    The Really Big Disaster, The Ripoff Queen,
    Scream Their Heads Off* (written by Leo
    Berenstain); *The Missing Merit Badges,
    The Search for Naughty Ned.*
Philadelphia Library CRRT Honor Book—*The
    Berenstain Bears: Big Bear, Small Bear.*

Web Award for Best Family Site—
    www.berenstainbears.com (Web Marketing
    Association).
Outstanding Alumni Awards: University of the Arts,
    Philadelphia (formerly Philadelphia Museum
    School of Industrial Art).

1999
Big Chapter Books with Leo and Michael Berenstain
    published: *The Berenstain Bears and the G-Rex
    Bones, The Berenstain Bears Go Hollywood,
    The Berenstain Bears in the Wax Museum,
    The Berenstain Bears: Lost in Cyberspace.*
*The Berenstain Bears' Mad, Mad, Mad Toy Craze*
    published.
*The Berenstain Bears Think of Those in Need,* with
    Michael Berenstain, published.
*The Berenstain Bears and the Big Question,* with
    Michael Berenstain, published.
*The Berenstain Bears Catch the Bus,* with Michael
    Berenstain, published.
*The Berenstain Bears Go Up and Down* published.
*The Berenstain Bears in the House of Mirrors*
    published.
Berenstain Baby Bears books with Michael Berenstain
    published: *My New Bed, My Potty and I,
    My Trusty Car Seat, Pacifier Days.*
The Berenstain Bear Scouts books, illustrated by
    Michael Berenstain, published: *The Stinky Milk
    Mystery, The Whitewater Mystery.*

2000
Big Chapter Books with Leo and Michael Berenstain
    published: *The Berenstain Bears and No Guns
    Allowed, The Berenstain Bears and the Great
    Ant Attack, The Berenstain Bears: Phenom in
    the Family.*
*The Berenstain Bears and Baby Makes Five* published.
*The Berenstain Bears and the Big Blooper,* with
    Michael Berenstain, published.
*The Birds, the Bees, and the Berenstain Bears*
    published.
*The Berenstain Bears and the Escape of the Bogg
    Brothers,* with Michael Berenstain, published.
*The Berenstain Bears Go In and Out* published.
*The Berenstain Bears: That Stump Must Go* published.

2001
*The Berenstain Bears and the Excuse Note* published.
*The Berenstain Bears' Dollars and Sense* published.
*The Berenstain Bears and the Missing Watermelon
    Money,* with Michael Berenstain, published.
*The Berenstain Bears and the Tic-Tac-Toe Mystery,*
    with Michael Berenstain, published.
Stepping Stone Books, illustrated by Michael
    Berenstain, published: *The Goofy, Goony Guy,
    The Haunted Lighthouse, The Runamuck Dog
    Show, The Wrong Crowd.*

2002
*The Berenstain Bears and the Real Easter Eggs*
    published.
*The Berenstain Bears' Report Card Trouble* published.
*Ride Like the Wind* published.

# INDEX